D1221162

ANGLICAN
LITURGIES

Edited by J. H. ARNOLD
FOR THE ALCUIN CLUB
OXFORD UNIVERSITY PRESS
LONDON : HUMPHREY MILFORD
1939

Extracts from the Prayer Book as proposed in 1928 have been reprinted by permission of the Prayer Book Copyright Committee of the Central Board of Finance of The Church of England.

The Liturgies indicated in brackets below are reprinted by kind permission of the following: Publications Committee of the Scottish Episcopal Church (Scottish); The Custodian of the Book of Common Prayer (American); The Episcopal Synod of the Church of the Province of South Africa (South African); the Rev. J. C. Winslow, and Messrs. Longmans, Green & Co., Ltd. (Indian); Archdeacon F. L. Beven (Ceylon).

The Dean of Chichester wishes to thank George Allen & Unwin Ltd. for permission to make use in his Foreword of some of the material contributed by him to *The New Prayer Book*.

FOREWORD

THE Reformation, it cannot be too often repeated, was a critical movement. In England this critical element showed itself most acute and discriminating in the sphere of public worship. The Prayer Book is the fruit of that criticism. It represents the efforts of many minds trained alike in study and in prayer, working over a long period, to recover for the people of England an order of prayer consistent with truth, faithful to the whole Catholic Church of Christ, calculated to excite piety and devotion, and tending to preserve the unity and peace of the Church. Nothing could show more clearly that the English liturgy is the fruit of a critical spirit than the fact that during one hundred and thirteen years it was revised four times; for we must regard the First Prayer Book, that of 1549, as itself a revision rather than the origination of an entirely new plan of worship.

In 1549 Cranmer attempted to retain in an English dress as much as possible of the old order that had been used in Western Europe for a thousand years. But it is important to notice that so far as the actual Anaphora was concerned, he greatly improved on his model. In place of a series of disjointed prayers, without logical sequence, he produced a noble eucharistic prayer moving in orderly progression from *Sursum Corda*, through Preface, Sanctus, Benedictus, the Intercession for the living and the dead, an Invocation of the Spirit, the Words of Institution, the Memorial before God, the offering of praise, and a prayer that the supplications of the Church may be accepted in Heaven, to a full close in the Lord's Prayer. This order was broken in 1552.

The most significant fact about the great prayer of 1549 is that it has always remained as an inspiration in the Anglican Communion. It is by no means true, as has been said, that there never has been any demand to restore the fuller Canon in place of our present mutilated version. In the first half of the seventeenth century a movement began with that object in view. In 1637 there was published for use in Scotland a Prayer Book based on the 1549 Book, which is generally known as 'Laud's Liturgy', though it was really drawn up by two Scottish Bishops, Maxwell of Ross and Wedderburn of Dunblane. But Laud's opinion of it is worth recalling: 'Though I shall not find fault with the order of the prayers, as they stand in the Communion-book of England (for, God be thanked, 'tis well); yet, if a comparison must be made, I do think the order of the prayers, as now they stand in the Scottish Liturgy, to be better, and more agreeable to use in the primitive Church; and I believe, they which are learned will acknowledge it.' Though 'Laud's Liturgy' failed to establish itself, it was not forgotten, and when the Episcopalians in Scotland desired to have a liturgy of their own, they took this as a basis. But they made one very significant change. Cranmer had introduced into his Consecration Prayer an Invocation of the Holy Spirit, probably for two reasons. Such an invocation occurs in the earliest account of the Eucharist that he knew (that of Justin Martyr), and is also to be found in the ancient Eastern liturgies and in some ancient non-Roman liturgies of the West. But he introduced it at a point unlike that at which it occurs there. He placed it before the Words of Institution, perhaps because he wished to introduce an Eastern feature without disturbing too greatly the later Western tradition, which had strangely come to connect consecration with the words with which our Lord administered the gifts to the Apostles. As 'Laud's Liturgy' came to be used, the impropriety of this arrangement became plain, and there sprang up a demand for what was rightly called 'The Natural Order'. Thus, when in 1764 an official liturgy was at last published by the Scottish Bishops, this natural order was introduced; the Invocation of the Holy Spirit came, by analogy with the Creed, after the recital of our Lord's redeeming work, and was not interjected into the middle of it, as it was in the First Prayer Book. In the 1764 liturgy, therefore, the blot in Cranmer's prayer was erased. The 'natural' order, the classical, the credal, the Trinitarian order, was reinstated.

It is important to notice how great throughout the Anglican Communion has been the influence of the liturgy of 1549, and how provincial is the view that imagines that the form in the Prayer Book of 1662 has found universal satisfaction. The Anglican Communion has grown to its present proportions and become a world-wide influence of great potential importance in Christendom. But it has done so, it must be confessed, in spite of the narrow and hide-bound conceptions that have often dominated the Church of England strictly so-called, the Church of the two provinces of Canterbury and York. In 1784 an event occurred that was destined to exercise a profound influence on the history of worship in the Anglican Communion. In that year, after many vain appeals to the English Bishops, Dr. Samuel Seabury was consecrated by Scottish Bishops in Aberdeen as the Bishop of Connecticut, the first Bishop of the American Church. At his consecration he entered into a solemn contract to model the American liturgy on that of Scotland. This in the main lines he did, and ever since, that great Church has had a Communion service that is in fact an improved edition of the First Prayer Book of King Edward VI. Thus in Scotland there has existed for more than two hundred years a liturgy much more like that of 1549 than that of 1662, and in the United States there is a Church with over a hundred diocesan Bishops of which the same may be said. It may be remarked in passing that though the same differences of emphasis exist in that Church as in ours, this noble form of consecration is used by all alike, High and Low, Conservative and Modernist.

But the whole tale is not told. Other Churches in the Anglican Communion have felt the same desire to substitute an improved version of 1549 for the abrupt Prayer of Consecration of 1662. During the first quarter of the twentieth century, a period sharply interrupted by the Great War, the Church in South Africa and the Church in India produced experimental revisions of their liturgies along the classical lines already followed in Scotland and America.

Meanwhile the revision movement in England had been strong. In 1927 and again in 1928 the Convocations of Canterbury and York gave their approval to an alternative Communion Service which followed the main structure and rhythm of the Scottish and American liturgies. Though not accepted by Parliament, the Bishops of the Church of England agreed in 1929, with the consent of the Lower Houses of Convocation, to allow the permissive use of this service.

In South Africa a period of experiment had been initiated in 1911 by a schedule of permitted modifications, and it was in order to assist in this process of revision that Dr. Frere wrote the essay which will be found at the end of this book. Of several revisions the final, which was given Synodical Confirmation in 1929, differs from all the other Anglican revisions based on the 1549 model in that it retains, as an interruption of the Recital of God's redemptive acts, the intrusive 'Hear us . . . ' prayer of 1552 (a petition that the receivers might partake of the Lord's Body and Blood) before the culminating Narrative of Institution.

In 1933 the Church of India, Burma, and Ceylon, followed in the same path by giving provincial authorization to an 'Indian Liturgy' which, though cast in an Oriental mode, adhered, so far as the Prayer of Consecration is concerned, to the principles that were embodied in the liturgies already referred to.

In 1938 the Indian Episcopate gave permission to the diocese of Colombo to use its own alternative Communion Service which in its general lines is nearer in character to the English revision of 1928, but owes some debt to the Indian Liturgy.

If all these revisions have shown themselves critical of the order of 1662, they have been no less so of that order of which eminent Roman Catholic scholars themselves have been frankly critical— the Roman Canon, the authoritative interpretation of which ties the moment of the consecration of the eucharist so firmly to the words *Hoc est corpus meum*. The movement in all the revisions, set forth in the pages which follow, has been away from such a rigid attributing of consecratory force to these words, or to any specific words. It has been a movement to get behind the idea of the utterance of a sacred and potent phrase, to the more Biblical and primitive conception of a process, in which the action of man is wholly subordinate to and dependent upon the Almighty Power of God; a solemn and thankful rehearsal before God of His redemptive work for man in its entirety, culminating in prayer and pleading and offering.

Taken as a whole, the eucharistic liturgies collected in this book have got behind East and West to that profoundly Christian state of mind, which looked on the whole action as consecratory, and did not think of pinning it down to a formula. It is sometimes said that we cannot make Easterns of Westerns. The new liturgies of the Anglican family do not attempt this impossible and unnecessary task. They endeavour to recapture the larger and truer ideas of an age that had not surrendered to the demands of an irrelevant logic. It is true that, in a sense, there must be a moment of consecration. But was not the old idea that the moment extended from the *Sursum Corda* to the Lord's Prayer, that the whole action was intensely solemn and awful, the true one? And, if it be true, need we despair of persuading people to accept it? May we not, indeed, be confident that it is an idea which, if faithfully taught, will find a ready echo in the consciences and hearts of Christian people generally?

A. S. DUNCAN-JONES

*   *   *

Information about rites which rest upon diocesan rather than synodical authority, and about translations of the Book of Common Prayer, will be found in the chapter 'Prayer Book Translations' of *Liturgy and Worship* (S.P.C.K.).

For invaluable guidance on the structure and history of the Eucharistic Prayer the reader is directed to Dr. W. H. Frere's *The Anaphora* (S.P.C.K.).

CONTENTS

THE ENGLISH RITE OF
1662

THE ORDER OF THE
ADMINISTRATION OF THE LORD'S SUPPER,

OR

HOLY COMMUNION

¶ *So many as intend to be partakers of the holy Communion shall signify their names to the Curate, at least some time the day before.*

¶ *And if any of those be an open and notorious evil liver, or have done any wrong to his neighbours by word or deed, so that the Congregation be thereby offended; the Curate, having knowledge thereof, shall call him and advertise him, that in any wise he presume not to come to the Lord's Table, until he have openly declared himself to have truly repented and amended his former naughty life, that the Congregation may thereby be satisfied, which before were offended; and that he have recompensed the parties, to whom he hath done wrong; or at least declare himself to be in full purpose so to do, as soon as he conveniently may.*

¶ *The same order shall the Curate use with those betwixt whom he perceiveth malice and hatred to reign; not suffering them to be partakers of the Lord's Table, until he know them to be reconciled. And if one of the parties so at variance be content to forgive from the bottom of his heart all that the other hath trespassed against him, and to make amends for that he himself hath offended; and the other party will not be persuaded to a godly unity, but remain still in his frowardness and malice: the Minister in that case ought to admit the penitent person to the holy Communion, and not him that is obstinate. Provided that every Minister so repelling any, as is specified in this, or the next precedent Paragraph of this Rubrick, shall be obliged to give an account of the same to the Ordinary within fourteen days after at the farthest. And the Ordinary shall proceed against the offending person according to the Canon.*

¶ *The Table, at the Communion-time having a fair white linen cloth upon it, shall stand in the Body of the Church, or in the Chancel, where Morning and Evening Prayer are appointed to be said. And the Priest standing at the north side of the Table shall say the Lord's Prayer, with the Collect following, the people kneeling.*

OUR Father which art in heaven, Hallowed be thy Name. Thy kingdom come. Thy will be done, in earth as it is in heaven. Give us this day our daily bread. And forgive us our trespasses, As we forgive them that trespass against us. And lead us not into temptation; But deliver us from evil. Amen.

3

The Collect.

ALMIGHTY God, unto whom all hearts be open, all desires known, and from whom no secrets are hid; Cleanse the thoughts of our hearts by the inspiration of thy Holy Spirit, that we may perfectly love thee, and worthily magnify thy holy Name; through Christ our Lord. *Amen.*

¶ *Then shall the Priest, turning to the people, rehearse distinctly all the TEN COMMANDMENTS; and the people still kneeling shall, after every Commandment, ask God mercy for their transgression thereof for the time past, and grace to keep the same for the time to come, as followeth.*

Minister.

GOD spake these words, and said; I am the Lord thy God: Thou shalt have none other gods but me.

People. Lord, have mercy upon us, and incline our hearts to keep this law.

Minister. Thou shalt not make to thyself any graven image, nor the likeness of any thing that is in heaven above, or in the earth beneath, or in the water under the earth. Thou shalt not bow down to them, nor worship them: for I the Lord thy God am a jealous God, and visit the sins of the fathers upon the children unto the third and fourth generation of them that hate me, and shew mercy unto thousands in them that love me, and keep my commandments.

People. Lord, have mercy upon us, and incline our hearts to keep this law.

Minister. Thou shalt not take the Name of the Lord thy God in vain: for the Lord will not hold him guiltless, that taketh his Name in vain.

People. Lord, have mercy upon us, and incline our hearts to keep this law.

Minister. Remember that thou keep holy the Sabbath-day. Six days shalt thou labour, and do all that thou hast to do; but the seventh day is the Sabbath of the Lord thy God. In it thou shalt do no manner of work, thou, and thy son, and thy daughter, thy man-servant, and thy maid-servant, thy cattle, and the stranger that is within thy gates.

4

For in six days the Lord made heaven and earth, the sea, and all that in them is, and rested the seventh day: wherefore the Lord blessed the seventh day, and hallowed it.

People. Lord, have mercy upon us, and incline our hearts to keep this law.

Minister. Honour thy father and thy mother; that thy days may be long in the land which the Lord thy God giveth thee.

People. Lord, have mercy upon us, and incline our hearts to keep this law.

Minister. Thou shalt do no murder.

People. Lord, have mercy upon us, and incline our hearts to keep this law.

Minister. Thou shalt not commit adultery.

People. Lord, have mercy upon us, and incline our hearts to keep this law.

Minister. Thou shalt not steal.

People. Lord, have mercy upon us, and incline our hearts to keep this law.

Minister. Thou shalt not bear false witness against thy neighbour.

People. Lord, have mercy upon us, and incline our hearts to keep this law.

Minister. Thou shalt not covet thy neighbour's house, thou shalt not covet thy neighbour's wife, nor his servant, nor his maid, nor his ox, nor his ass, nor any thing that is his.

People. Lord, have mercy upon us, and write all these thy laws in our hearts, we beseech thee.

¶ *Then shall follow one of these two Collects for the King, the Priest standing as before, and saying,*

Let us pray.

ALMIGHTY God, whose kingdom is everlasting, and power infinite; Have mercy upon the whole Church; and so rule the heart of thy chosen Servant *GEORGE*, our King and Governor, that he (knowing whose minister he is) may above all things seek thy honour and glory: and that we, and all his subjects (duly considering whose authority

5

he hath) may faithfully serve, honour, and humbly obey him, in thee, and for thee, according to thy blessed Word and ordinance; through Jesus Christ our Lord, who with thee and the Holy Ghost liveth and reigneth, ever one God, world without end. *Amen.*

Or,

ALMIGHTY and everlasting God, we are taught by thy holy Word, that the hearts of Kings are in thy rule and governance, and that thou dost dispose and turn them as it seemeth best to thy godly wisdom: We humbly beseech thee so to dispose and govern the heart of *GEORGE* thy Servant, our King and Governor, that, in all his thoughts, words, and works, he may ever seek thy honour and glory, and study to preserve thy people committed to his charge, in wealth, peace, and godliness: Grant this, O merciful Father, for thy dear Son's sake, Jesus Christ our Lord. *Amen.*

¶ *Then shall be said the Collect of the Day. And immediately after the Collect the Priest shall read the Epistle, saying,* The Epistle [*or,* The portion of Scripture appointed for the Epistle] is written in the —— Chapter of —— beginning at the —— Verse. *And the Epistle ended, he shall say,* Here endeth the Epistle. *Then shall he read the Gospel* (*the people all standing up*) *saying,* The holy Gospel is written in the —— Chapter of —— beginning at the —— Verse. *And the Gospel ended, shall be sung or said the Creed following, the people still standing, as before.*

I BELIEVE in one God the Father Almighty, Maker of heaven and earth, And of all things visible and invisible: And in one Lord Jesus Christ, the only-begotten Son of God, Begotten of his Father before all worlds, God of God, Light of Light, Very God of very God, Begotten, not made, Being of one substance with the Father, By whom all things were made: Who for us men, and for our salvation came down from heaven, And was incarnate by the Holy Ghost of the Virgin Mary, And was made man, And was crucified also for us under Pontius Pilate. He suffered and was buried, And the third day he rose again according to the Scriptures, And ascended into heaven, And sitteth on the right hand of the Father. And he shall come again with glory to judge both the quick and the dead: Whose kingdom shall have no end.

And I believe in the Holy Ghost, The Lord and giver of life, Who proceedeth from the Father and the Son, Who with the Father and the Son together is worshipped and glorified, Who spake by the Prophets. And I believe one Catholick and Apostolick Church. I acknowledge one Baptism for the remission of sins. And I look for the Resurrection of the dead, And the life of the world to come. Amen.

¶ *Then the Curate shall declare unto the people what Holy-days, or Fasting-days, are in the Week following to be observed. And then also (if occasion be) shall notice be given of the Communion; the Banns of Matrimony published, and Briefs, Citations, and Excommunications read. And nothing shall be proclaimed or published in the Church, during the time of Divine Service, but by the Minister: nor by him any thing, but what is prescribed in the Rules of this Book, or enjoined by the King, or by the Ordinary of the place.*

¶ *Then shall follow the Sermon, or one of the Homilies already set forth, or hereafter to be set forth, by authority.*

¶ *Then shall the Priest return to the Lord's Table, and begin the Offertory, saying one or more of these Sentences following, as he thinketh most convenient in his discretion.*

LET your light so shine before men, that they may see your good works, and glorify your Father which is in heaven. *St. Matth.* v.

Lay not up for yourselves treasure upon the earth; where the rust and moth doth corrupt, and where thieves break through and steal: but lay up for yourselves treasures in heaven; where neither rust nor moth doth corrupt, and where thieves do not break through and steal. *St. Matth.* vi.

Whatsoever ye would that men should do unto you, even so do unto them; for this is the Law and the Prophets. *St. Matth.* vii.

Not every one that saith unto me, Lord, Lord, shall enter into the Kingdom of heaven; but he that doeth the will of my Father which is in heaven. *St. Matth.* vii.

Zacchæus stood forth, and said unto the Lord, Behold, Lord, the half of my goods I give to the poor; and if I have done any wrong to any man, I restore four-fold. *St. Luke* xix.

Who goeth a warfare at any time of his own cost? Who planteth a vineyard, and eateth not of the fruit thereof? Or who feedeth a flock, and eateth not of the milk of the flock?

1 Cor. ix.

If we have sown unto you spiritual things, is it a great matter if we shall reap your worldly things? *1 Cor.* ix.

Do ye not know, that they who minister about holy things live of the sacrifice; and they who wait at the altar are partakers with the altar? Even so hath the Lord also ordained, that they who preach the Gospel should live of the Gospel.

1 Cor. ix.

He that soweth little shall reap little; and he that soweth plenteously shall reap plenteously. Let every man do according as he is disposed in his heart, not grudging, or of necessity; for God loveth a cheerful giver. *2 Cor.* ix.

Let him that is taught in the Word minister unto him that teacheth, in all good things. Be not deceived, God is not mocked: for whatsoever a man soweth that shall he reap.

Gal. vi.

While we have time, let us do good unto all men; and specially unto them that are of the household of faith.

Gal. vi.

Godliness is great riches, if a man be content with that he hath: for we brought nothing into the world, neither may we carry any thing out. *1 Tim.* vi.

Charge them who are rich in this world, that they be ready to give, and glad to distribute; laying up in store for themselves a good foundation against the time to come, that they may attain eternal life. *1 Tim.* vi.

God is not unrighteous, that he will forget your works, and labour that proceedeth of love; which love ye have shewed for his Name's sake, who have ministered unto the saints, and yet do minister. *Heb.* vi.

To do good, and to distribute, forget not; for with such sacrifices God is pleased. *Heb.* xiii.

Whoso hath this world's good, and seeth his brother have need, and shutteth up his compassion from him, how dwelleth the love of God in him? *1 St. John* iii.

Give alms of thy goods, and never turn thy face from any poor man; and then the face of the Lord shall not be turned away from thee. *Tobit* iv.

Be merciful after thy power. If thou hast much, give plenteously: if thou hast little, do thy diligence gladly to give of that little: for so gatherest thou thyself a good reward in the day of necessity. *Tobit* iv.

He that hath pity upon the poor lendeth unto the Lord: and look, what he layeth out, it shall be paid him again.
Prov. xix.

Blessed be the man that provideth for the sick and needy: the Lord shall deliver him in the time of trouble.
Psalm xli.

¶ *Whilst these Sentences are in reading, the Deacons, Church-wardens, or other fit person appointed for that purpose, shall receive the Alms for the Poor, and other devotions of the people, in a decent bason to be provided by the Parish for that purpose; and reverently bring it to the Priest, who shall humbly present and place it upon the holy Table.*

¶ *And when there is a Communion, the Priest shall then place upon the Table so much Bread and Wine, as he shall think sufficient. After which done, the Priest shall say,*

Let us pray for the whole state of Christ's Church militant here in earth.

ALMIGHTY and everliving God, who by thy holy Apostle hast taught us to make prayers, and supplications, and to give thanks, for all men; We humbly beseech thee most mercifully [*to accept our alms and oblations, and*] to receive these our prayers, which we offer unto thy Divine Majesty; beseeching thee to inspire con- ** If there be no alms or oblations, then shall the words [of accepting our alms and oblations] be left out unsaid.* tinually the universal Church with the spirit of truth, unity, and concord: And grant, that all they that do confess thy holy Name may agree in the truth of thy holy Word, and

9

live in unity, and godly love. We beseech thee also to save and defend all Christian Kings, Princes, and Governors; and specially thy Servant *GEORGE* our King; that under him we may be godly and quietly governed: And grant unto his whole Council, and to all that are put in authority under him, that they may truly and indifferently minister justice, to the punishment of wickedness and vice, and to the maintenance of thy true religion, and virtue. Give grace, O heavenly Father, to all Bishops and Curates, that they may both by their life and doctrine set forth thy true and lively Word, and rightly and duly administer thy holy Sacraments: And to all thy people give thy heavenly grace; and specially to this congregation here present; that, with meek heart and due reverence, they may hear, and receive thy holy Word; truly serving thee in holiness and righteousness all the days of their life. And we most humbly beseech thee of thy goodness, O Lord, to comfort and succour all them, who in this transitory life are in trouble, sorrow, need, sickness, or any other adversity. And we also bless thy holy Name for all thy servants departed this life in thy faith and fear; beseeching thee to give us grace so to follow their good examples, that with them we may be partakers of thy heavenly kingdom: Grant this, O Father, for Jesus Christ's sake, our only Mediator and Advocate. *Amen.*

¶ *When the Minister giveth warning for the celebration of the holy Communion, (which he shall always do upon the Sunday, or some Holy-day, immediately preceding,) after the Sermon or Homily ended, he shall read this Exhortation following.*

DEARLY beloved, on —— day next I purpose, through God's assistance, to administer to all such as shall be religiously and devoutly disposed the most comfortable Sacrament of the Body and Blood of Christ; to be by them received in remembrance of his meritorious Cross and Passion; whereby alone we obtain remission of our sins, and are made partakers of the Kingdom of heaven. Wherefore it is our duty to render most humble and hearty thanks to Almighty God our heavenly Father, for that he hath given his Son our Saviour Jesus Christ, not only to die for us, but also to be our spiritual food and sustenance in that holy Sacrament. Which being so divine and comfortable a thing to them who receive it worthily, and so dangerous to them that will presume to receive it unworthily; my duty is to exhort you in the mean season to consider the dignity of that holy mystery, and the great peril of the unworthy receiving thereof; and so to search and examine your own consciences, (and that not lightly, and after the manner of dissemblers with God; but so) that ye may come holy and clean to such a heavenly Feast, in the marriage-garment required by God in holy Scripture, and be received as worthy partakers of that holy Table.

The way and means thereto is; First, to examine your lives and conversations by the rule of God's commandments; and whereinsoever ye shall perceive yourselves to have offended, either by will, word, or deed, there to bewail your own sinfulness, and to confess yourselves to Almighty God, with full purpose of amendment of life. And if ye shall perceive your offences to be such as are not only against God, but also against your neighbours; then ye shall reconcile yourselves unto them; being ready to make restitution and satisfaction, according to the uttermost of your powers, for all injuries and wrongs done by you to any other; and being likewise ready to forgive others that have offended you, as ye would have forgiveness of your offences at God's hand: for otherwise the receiving of the holy Communion doth nothing else but increase your damnation. Therefore if any of you be a blasphemer of God, an hinderer or slanderer of his Word, an adulterer, or be in malice, or envy, or in any other grievous crime, repent you of your sins, or else come not to that holy Table; lest, after the taking of that holy Sacrament, the devil enter into you, as he entered into Judas, and fill you full of all iniquities, and bring you to destruction both of body and soul.

And because it is requisite, that no man should come to the holy Communion, but with a full trust in God's mercy, and with a quiet conscience; therefore if there be any of you, who by this means cannot quiet his own conscience herein, but requireth further comfort or counsel, let him come to me, or to some other discreet and learned Minister of God's Word, and open his grief; that by the ministry of God's holy Word he may receive the benefit of absolution, together with ghostly counsel and advice, to the quieting of his conscience, and avoiding of all scruple and doubtfulness.

¶ *Or, in case he shall see the people negligent to come to the holy Communion, instead of the former, he shall use this Exhortation.*

DEARLY beloved brethren, on ―― I intend, by God's grace, to celebrate the Lord's Supper: unto which, in God's behalf, I bid you all that are here present; and beseech you, for the Lord Jesus Christ's sake, that ye will not refuse to come thereto, being so lovingly called and bidden by God himself. Ye know how grievous and unkind a thing it is, when a man hath prepared a rich feast, decked his table with all kind of provision, so that there lacketh nothing but the guests to sit down; and yet they who are called (without any cause) most unthankfully refuse to come. Which of you in such a case would not be moved? Who would not think a great injury and wrong done unto him? Wherefore, most dearly beloved in Christ, take ye good heed, lest ye, withdrawing yourselves from this holy Supper, provoke God's indignation against you. It is an easy matter for a man to say, I will not communicate, because I am otherwise hindered with worldly business. But such excuses are not so easily accepted and allowed before God. If any man say, I am a grievous sinner, and therefore am afraid to come: wherefore then do ye not repent and amend? When God calleth you, are ye not ashamed to say ye will not come? When ye should return to God, will ye excuse yourselves, and say ye are not ready? Consider earnestly with yourselves how little such feigned excuses will avail before God. They that refused the feast in the Gospel, because they had bought a farm, or would try their yokes of oxen, or because they were married, were not so excused, but counted unworthy of the heavenly feast. I, for my part, shall be ready; and, according to mine Office, I bid you in the Name of God, I call you in Christ's behalf, I exhort you, as ye love your own salvation, that ye will be partakers of this holy Communion. And as the Son of God did vouchsafe to yield up his soul by death upon the Cross for your salvation; so it is your duty to receive the Communion in remembrance of the sacrifice of his death, as he himself hath commanded: which if ye shall neglect to do, consider with yourselves how great injury ye do unto God, and how sore punishment hangeth over your heads for the same; when ye wilfully abstain from the Lord's Table, and separate from your brethren, who come to feed on the banquet of that most heavenly food. These things if ye earnestly consider, ye will by God's grace return to a better mind: for the obtaining whereof we shall not cease to make our humble petitions unto Almighty God our heavenly Father.

¶ *At the time of the celebration of the Communion, the Communicants being conveniently placed for the receiving of the holy Sacrament, the Priest shall say this Exhortation.*

DEARLY beloved in the Lord, ye that mind to come to the holy Communion of the Body and Blood of our Saviour Christ, must consider how Saint Paul exhorteth all persons diligently to try and examine themselves, before they presume to eat of that Bread, and drink of that Cup. For as the benefit is great, if with a true penitent heart and lively faith we receive that holy Sacrament; (for then we spiritually eat the flesh of Christ, and drink his blood; then we dwell in Christ, and Christ in us; we are one with Christ, and Christ with us;) so is the danger great, if we receive the same unworthily. For then we are guilty of the Body and Blood of Christ our Saviour; we eat and drink our own damnation, not considering the Lord's Body; we kindle God's wrath against us; we provoke him to plague us with divers diseases, and sundry kinds of death. Judge therefore yourselves, brethren, that ye be not judged of the Lord; repent you truly for your sins past; have a lively and stedfast faith in Christ our Saviour; amend your lives, and be in perfect charity with all men; so shall ye be meet partakers of those holy mysteries. And above all things ye must give most humble and hearty thanks to God, the Father, the Son, and the Holy Ghost, for the redemption of the world by the death and passion of our Saviour Christ, both God and man; who did humble himself, even to the death upon the Cross, for us, miserable sinners, who lay in darkness and the shadow of death; that he might make us the children of God, and exalt us to everlasting life. And to the end that we should alway remember the exceeding great love of our Master, and only Saviour, Jesus Christ, thus dying for us, and the innumerable benefits which by his precious blood-shedding he hath obtained to us; he hath instituted and ordained holy mysteries, as pledges of his love, and for a continual remembrance of his death, to our great and endless comfort. To him therefore, with the Father and the Holy Ghost, let us give (as we are most bounden) continual thanks; submitting ourselves wholly to his holy will and pleasure, and studying to serve him in true holiness and righteousness all the days of our life. *Amen.*

¶ *Then shall the Priest say to them that come to receive the holy Communion,*

YE that do truly and earnestly repent you of your sins, and are in love and charity with your neighbours, and intend to lead a new life, following the commandments of God, and walking from henceforth in his holy ways; Draw near with faith, and take this holy Sacrament to your comfort; and make your humble confession to Almighty God, meekly kneeling upon your knees.

¶ *Then shall this general Confession be made, in the name of all those that are minded to receive the holy Communion, by one of the Ministers; both he and all the people kneeling humbly upon their knees, and saying,*

ALMIGHTY God, Father of our Lord Jesus Christ, Maker of all things, Judge of all men; We acknowledge and bewail our manifold sins and wickedness, Which we, from time to time, most grievously have committed, By thought, word, and deed, Against thy Divine Majesty, Provoking most justly thy wrath and indignation against us. We do earnestly repent, And are heartily sorry for these our misdoings; The remembrance of them is grievous unto us; The burden of them is intolerable. Have mercy upon us, Have mercy upon us, most merciful Father; For thy Son our Lord Jesus Christ's sake, Forgive us all that is past; And grant that we may ever hereafter Serve and please thee In newness of life, To the honour and glory of thy Name; Through Jesus Christ our Lord. Amen.

¶ *Then shall the Priest (or the Bishop, being present,) stand up, and turning himself to the people, pronounce this Absolution.*

ALMIGHTY God, our heavenly Father, who of his great mercy hath promised forgiveness of sins to all them that with hearty repentance and true faith turn unto him; Have mercy upon you; pardon and deliver you from all your sins; confirm and strengthen you in all goodness; and bring you to everlasting life; through Jesus Christ our Lord. *Amen.*

¶ *Then shall the Priest say,*

Hear what comfortable words our Saviour Christ saith unto all that truly turn to him.

COME unto me all that travail and are heavy laden, and I will refresh you. *St. Matth.* xi. 28.

So God loved the world, that he gave his only-begotten Son, to the end that all that believe in him should not perish, but have everlasting life. *St. John* iii. 16.

Hear also what Saint Paul saith.

This is a true saying, and worthy of all men to be received, That Christ Jesus came into the world to save sinners.

1 Tim. i. 15

Hear also what Saint John saith.

If any man sin, we have an Advocate with the Father, Jesus Christ the righteous; and he is the propitiation for our sins. *1 St. John* ii. 1.

¶ *After which the Priest shall proceed, saying,*

Lift up your hearts.

Answer. We lift them up unto the Lord.

Priest. Let us give thanks unto our Lord God.

Answer. It is meet and right so to do.

¶ *Then shall the Priest turn to the Lord's Table, and say,*

IT is very meet, right, and our bounden duty, that we should at all times, and in all places, give *These words [Holy thanks unto thee, O Lord, *Holy Father, Father] must be omitted on Trinity-Sunday. Almighty, Everlasting God.

These words [Holy Father] must be omitted on Trinity-Sunday.

¶ *Here shall follow the Proper Preface, according to the time, if there be any specially appointed: or else immediately shall follow,*

THEREFORE with Angels and Archangels, and with all the company of heaven, we laud and magnify thy glorious Name; evermore praising thee, and saying, Holy, holy, holy, Lord God of hosts, heaven and earth are full of thy glory: Glory be to thee, O Lord most High. Amen.

PROPER PREFACES

Upon Christmas-day, *and seven days after.*

BECAUSE thou didst give Jesus Christ thine only Son to be born as at this time for us; who, by the operation of the Holy Ghost, was made very man of the substance of the Virgin Mary his mother; and that without spot of sin, to make us clean from all sin. Therefore with Angels, &c.

Upon Easter-day, *and seven days after.*

BUT chiefly are we bound to praise thee for the glorious Resurrection of thy Son Jesus Christ our Lord: for he is the very Paschal Lamb, which was offered for us, and hath taken away the sin of the world; who by his death hath destroyed death, and by his rising to life again hath restored to us everlasting life. Therefore with Angels, &c.

Upon Ascension-day, *and seven days after.*

THROUGH thy most dearly beloved Son Jesus Christ our Lord; who after his most glorious Resurrection manifestly appeared to all his Apostles, and in their sight ascended up into heaven to prepare a place for us; that where he is, thither we might also ascend, and reign with him in glory. Therefore with Angels, &c.

Upon Whit-sunday, *and six days after.*

THROUGH Jesus Christ our Lord; according to whose most true promise, the Holy Ghost came down as at this time from heaven with a sudden great sound, as it had been a mighty wind, in the likeness of fiery tongues, lighting upon the Apostles, to teach them, and to lead them to all truth; giving them both the gift of divers languages, and also boldness with fervent zeal constantly to preach the Gospel unto all nations; whereby we have been brought out of darkness and error into the clear light and true knowledge of thee, and of thy Son Jesus Christ. Therefore with Angels, &c.

Upon the Feast of Trinity *only.*

WHO art one God, one Lord; not one only Person, but three Persons in one Substance. For that which we believe of the glory of the Father, the same we believe of the Son, and of the Holy Ghost, without any difference or inequality. Therefore with Angels, &c.

¶ *After each of which Prefaces shall immediately be sung or said,*

THEREFORE with Angels and Archangels, and with all the company of heaven, we laud and magnify thy glorious Name; evermore praising thee, and saying, Holy, holy, holy, Lord God of hosts, heaven and earth are full of thy glory: Glory be to thee, O Lord most High. Amen.

¶ *Then shall the Priest, kneeling down at the Lord's Table, say in the name of all them that shall receive the Communion this Prayer following.*

WE do not presume to come to this thy Table, O merciful Lord, trusting in our own righteousness, but in thy manifold and great mercies. We are not worthy so much as to gather up the crumbs under thy Table. But thou art the same Lord, whose property is always to have mercy: Grant us therefore, gracious Lord, so to eat the flesh of thy dear Son Jesus Christ, and to drink his blood, that our sinful bodies may be made clean by his body, and our souls washed through his most precious blood, and that we may evermore dwell in him, and he in us. *Amen.*

¶ *When the Priest, standing before the Table, hath so ordered the Bread and Wine, that he may with the more readiness and decency break the Bread before the people, and take the Cup into his hands, he shall say the Prayer of Consecration, as followeth.*

ALMIGHTY God, our heavenly Father, who of thy tender mercy didst give thine only Son Jesus Christ to suffer death upon the cross for our redemption; who made there (by his one oblation of himself once offered) a full, perfect, and sufficient sacrifice, oblation, and satisfaction, for the sins of the whole world; and did institute, and in his holy Gospel command us to continue, a perpetual memory of that his precious death, until his coming again; Hear us, O merciful Father, we most humbly beseech thee; and grant that we receiving these thy creatures of bread and wine, according to thy Son our Saviour Jesus Christ's holy institution, in remembrance of his death and passion, may be partakers of his most blessed Body and Blood: who, in the same night that he was betrayed, *a* took Bread; and, when he had given thanks, *b* he brake it, and gave it to his disciples, saying, Take, eat, *c* this is my Body which is given for you: Do this in remembrance of me. Likewise after supper he *d* took the Cup; and, when he had given thanks, he gave it to them, saying, Drink ye all of this; for this *e* is my Blood of the New Testament, which is shed for you and for many for the remission of sins: Do this, as oft as ye shall drink it, in remembrance of me. *Amen.*

a Here the Priest is to take the Paten into his hands:

b And here to break the Bread:

c And here to lay his hand upon all the Bread.

d Here he is to take the Cup into his hand:

e And here to lay his hand upon every vessel (be it Chalice or Flagon) in which there is any Wine to be consecrated.

¶ *Then shall the Minister first receive the Communion in both kinds himself, and then proceed to deliver the same to the Bishops, Priests, and Deacons, in like manner, (if any be present,) and after that to the people also in order, into their hands, all meekly kneeling. And, when he delivereth the Bread to any one, he shall say,*

THE Body of our Lord Jesus Christ, which was given for thee, preserve thy body and soul unto everlasting life. Take and eat this in remembrance that Christ died for thee, and feed on him in thy heart by faith with thanksgiving.

¶ And the Minister that delivereth the Cup to any one shall say,

THE Blood of our Lord Jesus Christ, which was shed for thee, preserve thy body and soul unto everlasting life. Drink this in remembrance that Christ's Blood was shed for thee, and be thankful.

¶ If the consecrated Bread or Wine be all spent before all have communicated, the Priest is to consecrate more according to the Form before prescribed; beginning at [Our Saviour Christ in the same night, &c.] for the blessing of the Bread; and at [Likewise after Supper, &c.] for the blessing of the Cup.

¶ When all have communicated, the Minister shall return to the Lord's Table, and reverently place upon it what remaineth of the consecrated Elements, covering the same with a fair linen cloth.

¶ Then shall the Priest say the Lord's Prayer, the people repeating after him every Petition.

OUR Father, which art in heaven, Hallowed be thy Name. Thy kingdom come. Thy will be done, in earth as it is in heaven. Give us this day our daily bread. And forgive us our trespasses, As we forgive them that trespass against us. And lead us not into temptation; But deliver us from evil: For thine is the kingdom, The power, and the glory, For ever and ever. Amen.

¶ After shall be said as followeth.

O LORD and heavenly Father, we thy humble servants entirely desire thy fatherly goodness mercifully to accept this our sacrifice of praise and thanksgiving; most humbly beseeching thee to grant, that by the merits and death of thy Son Jesus Christ, and through faith in his blood, we and all thy whole Church may obtain remission of our sins, and all other benefits of his passion. And here we offer and present unto thee, O Lord, ourselves, our souls and bodies, to be a reasonable, holy, and lively sacrifice unto thee; humbly beseeching thee, that all we, who are partakers of this holy Communion, may be fulfilled with thy grace and heavenly benediction. And although we be unworthy, through our manifold sins, to offer unto thee any sacrifice, yet we beseech thee to accept this our bounden duty and service; not weighing our merits, but pardoning our offences, through Jesus Christ our Lord; by whom, and with whom, in the unity of the Holy Ghost, all honour and glory be unto thee, O Father Almighty, world without end. *Amen.*

Or this.

ALMIGHTY and everliving God, we most heartily thank thee, for that thou dost vouchsafe to feed us, who have duly received these holy mysteries, with the spiritual food of the most precious Body and Blood of thy Son our Saviour Jesus Christ; and dost assure us thereby of thy favour and goodness towards us; and that we are very members incorporate in the mystical body of thy Son, which is the blessed company of all faithful people; and are also heirs through hope of thy everlasting kingdom, by the merits of the most precious death and passion of thy dear Son. And we most humbly beseech thee, O heavenly Father, so to assist us with thy grace, that we may continue in that holy fellowship, and do all such good works as thou hast prepared for us to walk in; through Jesus Christ our Lord, to whom, with thee and the Holy Ghost, be all honour and glory, world without end. *Amen.*

¶ *Then shall be said or sung,*

GLORY be to God on high, and in earth peace, good will towards men. We praise thee, we bless thee, we worship thee, we glorify thee, we give thanks to thee for thy great glory, O Lord God, heavenly King, God the Father Almighty.

O Lord, the only-begotten Son Jesu Christ; O Lord God, Lamb of God, Son of the Father, that takest away the sins of the world, have mercy upon us. Thou that takest away the sins of the world, have mercy upon us. Thou that takest away the sins of the world, receive our prayer. Thou that sittest at the right hand of God the Father, have mercy upon us.

For thou only art holy; thou only art the Lord; thou only, O Christ, with the Holy Ghost, art most high in the glory of God the Father. Amen.

20

¶ *Then the Priest (or Bishop if he be present) shall let them depart with this Blessing.*

THE peace of God, which passeth all understanding, keep your hearts and minds in the knowledge and love of God, and of his Son Jesus Christ our Lord: and the blessing of God Almighty, the Father, the Son, and the Holy Ghost, be amongst you and remain with you always. *Amen.*

¶ *Collects to be said after the Offertory, when there is no Communion, every such day one or more; and the same may be said also, as often as occasion shall serve, after the Collects either of Morning or Evening Prayer, Communion, or Litany, by the discretion of the Minister.*

ASSIST us mercifully, O Lord, in these our supplications and prayers, and dispose the way of thy servants towards the attainment of everlasting salvation; that, among all the changes and chances of this mortal life, they may ever be defended by thy most gracious and ready help; through Jesus Christ our Lord. *Amen.*

O ALMIGHTY Lord, and everlasting God, vouchsafe, we beseech thee, to direct, sanctify, and govern, both our hearts and bodies, in the ways of thy laws, and in the works of thy commandments; that through thy most mighty protection, both here and ever, we may be preserved in body and soul; through our Lord and Saviour Jesus Christ. *Amen.*

GRANT, we beseech thee, Almighty God, that the words, which we have heard this day with our outward ears, may through thy grace be so grafted inwardly in our hearts, that they may bring forth in us the fruit of good living, to the honour and praise of thy Name; through Jesus Christ our Lord. *Amen.*

PREVENT us, O Lord, in all our doings with thy most gracious favour, and further us with thy continual help; that in all our works begun, continued, and ended in thee, we may glorify thy holy Name, and finally by thy mercy obtain everlasting life; through Jesus Christ our Lord. *Amen.*

ALMIGHTY God, the fountain of all wisdom, who knowest our necessities before we ask, and our ignorance in asking; We beseech thee to have compassion upon our infirmities; and those things, which for our unworthiness we dare not, and for our blindness we cannot ask, vouchsafe to give us, for the worthiness of thy Son Jesus Christ our Lord. *Amen.*

ALMIGHTY God, who hast promised to hear the petitions of them that ask in thy Son's Name; We beseech thee mercifully to incline thine ears to us that have made now our prayers and supplications unto thee; and grant, that those things, which we have faithfully asked according to thy will, may effectually be obtained, to the relief of our necessity, and to the setting forth of thy glory; through Jesus Christ our Lord. *Amen.*

¶ *Upon the Sundays and other Holy-days (if there be no Communion) shall be said all that is appointed at the Communion, until the end of the general Prayer* [For the whole state of Christ's Church militant here in earth] *together with one or more of these Collects last before rehearsed, concluding with the Blessing.*

¶ *And there shall be no celebration of the Lord's Supper, except there be a convenient number to communicate with the Priest, according to his discretion.*

¶ *And if there be not above twenty persons in the Parish of discretion to receive the Communion; yet there shall be no Communion, except four (or three at the least) communicate with the Priest.*

¶ *And in Cathedral and Collegiate Churches, and Colleges, where there are many Priests and Deacons, they shall all receive the Communion with the Priest every Sunday at the least, except they have a reasonable cause to the contrary.*

¶ *And to take away all occasion of dissension and superstition, which any person hath or might have concerning the Bread and Wine, it shall suffice that the Bread be such as is usual to be eaten; but the best and purest Wheat Bread that conveniently may be gotten.*

¶ *And if any of the Bread and Wine remain unconsecrated, the Curate shall have it to his own use: but if any remain of that which was consecrated, it shall not be carried out of the Church, but the Priest and such other of the Communicants as he shall then call unto him, shall, immediately after the Blessing, reverently eat and drink the same.*

¶ *The Bread and Wine for the Communion shall be provided by the Curate and the Church-wardens at the charges of the Parish.*

¶ *And note, that every Parishioner shall communicate at the least three times in the year, of which Easter to be one. And yearly at Easter every Parishioner shall reckon with the Parson, Vicar, or Curate, or his or their Deputy or Deputies; and pay to them or him all Ecclesiastical Duties, accustomably due, then and at that time to be paid.*

¶ *After the Divine Service ended, the money given at the Offertory shall be disposed of to such pious and charitable uses, as the Minister and Church-wardens shall think fit. Wherein if they disagree, it shall be disposed of as the Ordinary shall appoint.*

¶ *Whereas it is ordained in this Office for the Administration of the Lord's Supper, that the Communicants should receive the same kneeling; (which order is well meant, for a signification of our humble and grateful acknowledgement of the benefits of Christ therein given to all worthy Receivers, and for the avoiding of such profanation and disorder in the holy Communion, as might otherwise ensue;) yet, lest the same kneeling should by any persons, either out of ignorance and infirmity, or out of malice and obstinacy, be misconstrued and depraved; It is hereby declared, That thereby no adoration is intended, or ought to be done, either unto the Sacramental Bread or Wine there bodily received, or unto any Corporal Presence of Christ's natural Flesh and Blood. For the Sacramental Bread and Wine remain still in their very natural substances, and therefore may not be adored; (for that were Idolatry, to be abhorred of all faithful Christians;) and the natural Body and Blood of our Saviour Christ are in Heaven, and not here; it being against the truth of Christ's natural Body to be at one time in more places than one.*

THE ENGLISH RITE OF
1928

'AN ALTERNATIVE ORDER FOR THE
ADMINISTRATION OF THE LORD'S
SUPPER OR HOLY COMMUNION'
AS PROPOSED IN 1928

GENERAL RUBRICKS [1]

OF THE

ADMINISTRATION OF THE LORD'S SUPPER

OR

HOLY COMMUNION

¶ *It is convenient that so many as intend to be partakers of the Holy Communion should signify their names to the Curate.*

¶ *If any be an open and notorious evil liver, or have done any wrong to his neighbours by word or deed, so that the Congregation be thereby offended; the Curate, having knowledge thereof, shall call him and advertise him, that in any wise he presume not to come to the Lord's Table, until he have openly declared himself to have truly repented and amended his former naughty life, that the Congregation may thereby be satisfied, which before were offended; and that he have recompensed the parties, to whom he hath done wrong; or at least declare himself to be in full purpose so to do, as soon as he conveniently may.*

¶ *The same order shall the Curate use with those betwixt whom he perceiveth malice and hatred to reign; not suffering them to be partakers of the Lord's Table, until he know them to be reconciled. And if one of the parties so at variance be content to forgive from the bottom of his heart all that the other hath trespassed against him, and to make amends for that he himself hath offended; and the other party will not be persuaded to a godly unity, but remain still in his frowardness and malice: the Minister in that case ought to admit the penitent person to the Holy Communion, and not him that is obstinate.*

¶ *Provided that every Minister so advertising or repelling any, as is specified in the two next precedent paragraphs, shall be obliged forthwith to give an account of the same to the Bishop, and therein to obey his order and direction.*

¶ *The Service following shall be said throughout in a distinct and audible voice.*

¶ *The Order here provided shall not be supplemented by additional prayers, save so far as is herein permitted; nor shall the private devotions of the Priest be such as to hinder, interrupt, or alter the course of the Service.*

¶ *There shall be no celebration of the Lord's Supper, except there be a convenient number to communicate with the Priest according to his discretion.*

---

[1] In Prayer Books containing the rites of 1662 and 1928, these rubrics precede the rite of 1662, from which the initial rubrics (p. 3) are omitted except the last sentence; similarly the final rubrics (pp. 22, 23) except the first, sixth, and last. Side rules call attention to modifications of the Order of 1662 or to new material.

¶ It is much to be wished that at every celebration of the Lord's Supper the worshippers present, not being reasonably hindered, will communicate with the Priest.

¶ And in Cathedral and Collegiate Churches, and Colleges, where there are many Priests and Deacons, they shall all receive the Communion with the Priest every Sunday at the least, except they have a reasonable cause to the contrary.

¶ Every confirmed member of the Church shall communicate at the least three times in the year, of which Easter to be one.

¶ It is an ancient and laudable custom of the Church to receive this Holy Sacrament fasting. Yet for the avoidance of all scruple it is hereby declared that such preparation may be used or not used, according to every man's conscience in the sight of God.

¶ For the avoidance of all controversy and doubtfulness, it is hereby prescribed that, notwithstanding anything that is elsewhere enjoined in any Rubric or Canon, the Priest, in celebrating the Holy Communion, shall wear either a surplice with stole or with scarf and hood, or a white alb plain with a vestment or cope.

¶ The Table, at the Communion-time having a fair white linen cloth upon it, shall stand in the body of the church, or in the chancel, where Morning and Evening Prayer are appointed to be said.

¶ To take away all occasion of dissension and superstition which any person hath or might have concerning the Bread and Wine, it shall suffice that the Bread be such as is usual to be eaten. And it is desirable that the Bread shall be the best and purest wheat bread, whether loaf or wafer, that conveniently may be gotten. The Bread and Wine for the Communion shall be provided by the Curate and the Churchwardens of the Parish.

¶ If the consecrated Bread and Wine be all spent before all have communicated, the Priest is to consecrate more according to the form prescribed.

¶ After the Service ended, the money given at the Offertory shall be disposed of to such pious and charitable uses as the Curate and Churchwardens shall think fit. Wherein if they disagree, it shall be disposed of as the Bishop shall appoint.

¶ Yearly at Easter every parishioner shall reckon with the Parson, Vicar, or Curate, or his or their deputy or deputies; and pay to them or him all ecclesiastical duties accustomably due then and at that time to be paid.

¶ From the Comfortable Words until the Blessing the Service shall follow continuously one or other of the two Orders here ensuing without any interchange, but it shall be permissible in using the Order of 1662 to adopt any of the Proper Prefaces, or of the methods of administration sanctioned in the Alternative Order.

¶ The Minister of a Parish shall celebrate the Holy Communion according to the Order of 1662 on at least one Sunday in each month in any case where either the Parochial Church Council so desires or the Bishop of the Diocese, being satisfied that there is a substantial desire in the Parish for a celebration according to the said Order, so directs.

28

AN ALTERNATIVE ORDER FOR THE
ADMINISTRATION OF THE LORD'S SUPPER

OR

HOLY COMMUNION
(1928)

¶ The Priest standing at God's Board shall say the Lord's Prayer with the Collect following, the people kneeling.

THE INTRODUCTION

OUR Father, which art in heaven, Hallowed be thy name; Thy kingdom come; Thy will be done; In earth as it is in heaven. Give us this day our daily bread. And forgive us our trespasses, As we forgive them that trespass against us. And lead us not into temptation; But deliver us from evil. Amen.

The Collect.

ALMIGHTY God, unto whom all hearts be open, all desires known, and from whom no secrets are hid: Cleanse the thoughts of our hearts by the inspiration of thy Holy Spirit, that we may perfectly love thee, and worthily magnify thy holy name; through Christ our Lord. *Amen.*

¶ Then shall the Priest, turning to the people, rehearse distinctly all the TEN COMMANDMENTS; and the people, still kneeling, shall after every commandment ask God mercy for their transgression of every duty therein (either according to the letter or according to the spiritual import thereof) for the time past, and grace to keep the same for the time to come, as followeth.

Priest. God spake these words and said:

I am the Lord thy God; thou shalt have none other gods but me.

People. Lord, have mercy upon us, and incline our hearts to keep this law.

Priest. Thou shalt not make to thyself any graven image, nor the likeness of any thing that is in heaven above, or in

29

the earth beneath, or in the water under the earth. Thou shalt not bow down to them, nor worship them.

People. Lord, have mercy upon us, and incline our hearts to keep this law.

Priest. Thou shalt not take the name of the Lord thy God in vain.

People. Lord, have mercy upon us, and incline our hearts to keep this law.

Priest. Remember that thou keep holy the Sabbath day. Six days shalt thou labour, and do all that thou hast to do; but the seventh day is the Sabbath of the Lord thy God.

People. Lord, have mercy upon us, and incline our hearts to keep this law.

Priest. Honour thy father and thy mother.

People. Lord, have mercy upon us, and incline our hearts to keep this law.

Priest. Thou shalt do no murder.

People. Lord, have mercy upon us, and incline our hearts to keep this law.

Priest. Thou shalt not commit adultery.

People. Lord, have mercy upon us, and incline our hearts to keep this law.

Priest. Thou shalt not steal.

People. Lord, have mercy upon us, and incline our hearts to keep this law.

Priest. Thou shalt not bear false witness.

People. Lord, have mercy upon us, and incline our hearts to keep this law.

Priest. Thou shalt not covet.

People. Lord, have mercy upon us, and write all these thy laws in our hearts, we beseech thee.

The Ten Commandments may be omitted, provided that they be rehearsed at least once on a Sunday in each month: and when they are so omitted, then shall be said in place thereof our Lord's Summary of the Law.

Priest. Our Lord Jesus Christ said: Hear O Israel, The Lord our God is one Lord; and thou shalt love the Lord thy God with all thy heart, and with all thy soul, and with all thy mind, and with all thy strength. This is the first commandment. And the second is like, namely this: Thou shalt love thy neighbour as thyself. There is none other commandment greater than these. On these two commandments hang all the Law and the Prophets.

Answer. Lord, have mercy upon us, and incline our hearts to keep this law.

Or else the following may be sung or said.

Lord, have mercy.		Kyrie, eleison.
Christ, have mercy.	or,	*Christe, eleison.*
Lord, have mercy.		Kyrie, eleison.

The Ten Commandments or else the Summary shall be said on Sundays. At other times, instead thereof, the following may be sung or said.

Lord, have mercy.		Kyrie, eleison.
Christ, have mercy.	or,	*Christe, eleison.*
Lord, have mercy.		Kyrie, eleison.

¶ *Then the Priest standing as before, shall say,*

The Lord be with you;
Answer. And with thy spirit.

Let us pray.

¶ *And turning to the Holy Table he shall say the Collect of the Day. Other Collects contained in this Book or authorized by the Bishop may follow.*

THE MINISTRY OF THE WORD

¶ *Immediately thereafter he that readeth the Epistle shall say,* The Epistle [or The Lesson] is written in the —— chapter of —— beginning at the —— verse. *And the reading ended, he shall say,* Here endeth the Epistle [or the Lesson].

¶ *Then the Deacon or Priest that readeth the Gospel (the people all standing up) shall say,* The Holy Gospel is written in the —— chapter of the Gospel according to Saint ——, beginning at the —— verse.

Answer. Glory be to thee, O Lord.

And the Gospel shall be read.

He that readeth the Epistle or the Gospel shall so stand and turn himself as he may best be heard of the people.

The Gospel ended, there may be said,

Praise be to thee, O Christ.

31

¶ Then shall be sung or said the Creed following, the people still standing as before: except that at the discretion of the Minister it may be omitted on any day not being a Sunday or a Holy-day.

I BELIEVE in one God the Father Almighty, Maker of heaven and earth, And of all things visible and invisible:
And in one Lord Jesus Christ, the only-begotten Son of God, Begotten of his Father before all worlds, God of God, Light of Light, Very God of very God, Begotten, not made, Being of one substance with the Father, By whom all things were made: Who for us men, and for our salvation came down from heaven, And was incarnate by the Holy Ghost of the Virgin Mary, And was made man, And was crucified also for us under Pontius Pilate. He suffered and was buried, And the third day he rose again according to the Scriptures, And ascended into heaven, And sitteth on the right hand of the Father. And he shall come again with glory to judge both the quick and the dead: Whose kingdom shall have no end.

And I believe in the Holy Ghost, The Lord, The giver of life, Who proceedeth from the Father and the Son, Who with the Father and the Son together is worshipped and glorified, Who spake by the Prophets.

And I believe One Holy Catholick and Apostolick Church. I acknowledge one Baptism for the remission of sins. And I look for the Resurrection of the dead, And the Life of the world to come. Amen.

¶ Then the Curate shall declare unto the people what Holy-days or Fasting Days are in the week following to be observed. And then also, if occasion be, shall notice be given of the Holy Communion, or of other Services; Banns of matrimony may be published, and Briefs, Citations, and Excommunications shall be read, and Bidding of Prayers may be made. And nothing shall be proclaimed or published in the church during the time of Service, but by the Minister: nor by him any thing but what is prescribed in the rules of this Book, or enjoined by the King, or enjoined or permitted by the Bishop.

¶ Then may follow the Sermon, or one of the Homilies already set forth, or hereafter to be set forth, by authority.

¶ When the Minister giveth warning for the celebration of the Holy Communion, he may read to the people, at such times as he shall think convenient, one of the two Exhortations placed at the end of this Order.

THE OFFERTORY

¶ *Then shall the Priest, standing at the Lord's Table, begin the Offertory, saying one or more of these Sentences following, as he thinketh most convenient in his discretion, or the Priests and Clerks shall sing the same.*

LET your light so shine before men, that they may see your good works, and glorify your Father which is in heaven. *St. Matthew* 5. 16.

Lay not up for yourselves treasure upon the earth; where the rust and moth doth corrupt, and where thieves break through and steal: but lay up for yourselves treasures in heaven; where neither rust nor moth doth corrupt, and where thieves do not break through and steal. *St. Matthew* 6. 19.

Whatsoever ye would that men should do unto you, even so do unto them; for this is the Law and the Prophets. *St. Matthew* 7. 12.

Not every one that saith unto me, Lord, Lord, shall enter into the kingdom of heaven; but he that doeth the will of my Father which is in heaven. *St. Matthew* 7. 21.

Remember the words of the Lord Jesus, how he said, It is more blessed to give than to receive. *Acts* 20. 35.

Godliness is great riches, if a man be content with that he hath: for we brought nothing into the world, neither may we carry any thing out. 1 *Timothy* 6. 6.

Be merciful after thy power. If thou hast much, give plenteously: if thou hast little, do thy diligence gladly to give of that little: for so gatherest thou thyself a good reward in the day of necessity. *Tobit* 4. 8.

All things come of thee, and of thine own have we given thee. 1 *Chronicles* 29. 14.

If we have sown unto you spiritual things, is it a great matter if we shall reap your worldly things? 1 *Corinthians* 9. 11.

Do ye not know, that they who minister about holy things live of the sacrifice; and they who wait at the altar are partakers with the altar? Even so hath the Lord also ordained, that they who preach the Gospel should live of the Gospel. 1 *Corinthians* 9. 13.

He that soweth little shall reap little; and he that soweth plenteously shall reap plenteously. Let every man do according as he is disposed in his heart, not grudging, or of necessity; for God loveth a cheerful giver. *2 Corinthians* 9. 6.

Let him that is taught in the Word minister unto him that teacheth, in all good things. Be not deceived, God is not mocked: for whatsoever a man soweth that shall he reap. *Galatians* 6. 6.

While we have time, let us do good unto all men; and specially unto them that are of the household of faith. *Galatians* 6. 10.

God is not unrighteous, that he will forget your works, and labour that proceedeth of love; which love ye have shewed for his name's sake, who have ministered unto the saints, and yet do minister. *Hebrews* 6. 10.

Lift up your eyes and look upon the fields; for they are white already to harvest. *St. John* 4. 35.

Charge them who are rich in this world, that they be ready to give, and glad to distribute; laying up in store for themselves a good foundation against the time to come, that they may attain eternal life. *1 Timothy* 6. 17.

Whoso hath this world's good, and seeth his brother have need, and shutteth up his compassion from him, how dwelleth the love of God in him? *1 St. John* 3. 17.

Blessed be the man that provideth for the sick and needy: the Lord shall deliver him in the time of trouble. *Psalm* 41. 1.

To do good, and to distribute, forget not; for with such sacrifices God is pleased. *Hebrews* 13. 16.

Offer unto God thanksgiving, and pay thy vows unto the most Highest. *Psalm* 50. 14.

I will offer in his dwelling an oblation with great gladness: I will sing and speak praises unto the Lord. *Psalm* 27. 6.

Melchizedek king of Salem brought forth bread and wine; and he was the priest of the most high God. *Genesis* 14. 18.

34

¶ *While these Sentences are said or sung, the Deacons, Churchwardens, or other fit persons appointed for that purpose, shall receive the alms for the poor, or other devotions of the people, and reverently bring them to the Priest, who shall humbly present and place them upon the Holy Table in a decent bason to be provided for that purpose.*

¶ *And when there is a Communion, the Priest shall place upon the Holy Table so much Bread and Wine, as he shall think sufficient.*

¶ *It is an ancient tradition of the Church to mingle a little water with the wine.*

¶ *The Priest may here bid special prayers and thanksgivings.*

¶ *Then he shall begin the Intercession.*

THE INTERCESSION

Let us pray for the whole state of Christ's Church.

ALMIGHTY and everliving God, who by thy holy Apostle hast taught us to make prayers, and supplications, and to give thanks, for all men: We humbly beseech thee most mercifully [*to accept our alms and oblations, and*] to receive these our prayers, which we offer unto thy Divine Majesty; beseeching thee to inspire con-

* If there be no alms or oblations, then shall the words [of accepting our alms and oblations] be left out unsaid.

tinually the universal Church with the spirit of truth, unity, and concord: And grant, that all they that do confess thy holy name may agree in the truth of thy holy Word, and live in unity, and godly love.

We beseech thee also to lead all nations in the way of righteousness and peace; and so to direct all kings and rulers, that under them thy people may be godly and quietly governed. And grant unto thy servant *GEORGE* our King, and to all that are put in authority under him, that they may truly and impartially minister justice, to the punishment of wickedness and vice, and to the maintenance of thy true religion, and virtue.

Give grace, O heavenly Father, to all Bishops, Priests, and Deacons, especially to thy servant *N.* our bishop, that they may both by their life and doctrine set forth thy true and living Word and rightly and duly administer thy Holy Sacraments.

35

Guide and prosper, we pray thee, those who are labouring for the spread of thy Gospel among the nations, and enlighten with thy Spirit all places of education and learning; that the whole world may be filled with the knowledge of thy truth.

And to all thy people give thy heavenly grace; and specially to this congregation here present; that, with meek heart and due reverence, they may hear, and receive thy holy Word; truly serving thee in holiness and righteousness all the days of their life.

And we most humbly beseech thee of thy goodness, O Lord, to comfort and succour all them, who in this transitory life are in trouble, sorrow, need, sickness, or any other adversity.

And we commend to thy gracious keeping, O Lord, all thy servants departed this life in thy faith and fear, beseeching thee to grant them everlasting light and peace.

And here we give thee most high praise and hearty thanks for all thy Saints, who have been the chosen vessels of thy grace, and lights of the world in their several generations; and we pray, that rejoicing in their fellowship, and following their good examples, we may be partakers with them of thy heavenly kingdom.

Grant this, O Father, for Jesus Christ's sake, our only Mediator and Advocate; who liveth and reigneth with thee in the unity of the Holy Ghost, one God, world without end. *Amen.*

THE PREPARATION

¶ *At the time of the celebration of the Holy Communion, the communicants being conveniently placed for the receiving of the Holy Sacrament, the Priest may say this Exhortation. And if this Exhortation be not read at the time of the celebration of the Holy Communion, it shall nevertheless be read to the people by the Curate at such times as he think fit, and at the least on either the fourth or fifth Sunday in Lent.*

DEARLY beloved in the Lord, ye that mind to come to the Holy Communion of the Body and Blood of our Saviour Christ, must consider how Saint Paul exhorteth all persons diligently to try and examine themselves, before they presume to eat of that Bread, and drink of that Cup.

For as the benefit is great, if with a true penitent heart and lively faith we receive that Holy Sacrament; (for then we spiritually eat the flesh of Christ, and drink his blood; then we dwell in Christ, and Christ in us; we are one with Christ, and Christ with us;) so is the danger great, if we receive the same unworthily. For then we are guilty of the Body and Blood of Christ our Saviour.

Judge therefore yourselves, brethren, that ye be not judged of the Lord; repent you truly for your sins past; have a lively and stedfast faith in Christ our Saviour; amend your lives, and be in perfect charity with all men; so shall ye be meet partakers of those holy mysteries.

And above all things ye must give most humble and hearty thanks to God, the Father, the Son, and the Holy Ghost, for the redemption of the world by the death and passion of our Saviour Christ, both God and man; who did humble himself, even to the death upon the Cross, for us, miserable sinners, who lay in darkness and the shadow of death; that he might make us the children of God, and exalt us to everlasting life.

And to the end that we should alway remember the exceeding great love of our Master, and only Saviour, Jesus Christ, thus dying for us, and the innumerable benefits which by his precious blood-shedding he hath obtained to us; he hath instituted and ordained holy mysteries, as pledges of his love, and for a continual remembrance of his death, to our great and endless comfort.

To him therefore, with the Father and the Holy Ghost, let us give (as we are most bounden) continual thanks; submitting ourselves wholly to his holy will and pleasure, and studying to serve him in true holiness and righteousness all the days of our life. *Amen.*

¶ *Then shall the Minister say to them that come to receive the Holy Communion,*

YE that do truly and earnestly repent you of your sins, and are in love and charity with your neighbours, and intend to lead a new life, following the commandments of God, and walking from henceforth in his holy ways; Draw near with faith, and take this Holy Sacrament to your comfort; and make your humble confession to Almighty God, meekly kneeling upon your knees.

Then shall this general Confession be begun, in the name of all those that are minded to receive the Holy Communion, by the Priest or one of the Ministers; both he and all the people kneeling humbly upon their knees, and saying,

ALMIGHTY God, Father of our Lord Jesus Christ, Maker of all things, Judge of all men: We acknowledge and bewail our manifold sins and wickedness, Which we, from time to time, most grievously have committed, By thought, word, and deed, Against thy Divine Majesty, Provoking most justly thy wrath and indignation against us. We do earnestly repent, And are heartily sorry for these our misdoings; The remembrance of them is grievous unto us; The burden of them is intolerable. Have mercy upon us, Have mercy upon us, most merciful Father; For thy Son our Lord Jesus Christ's sake, Forgive us all that is past; And grant that we may ever hereafter Serve and please thee In newness of life, To the honour and glory of thy name; Through Jesus Christ our Lord. Amen.

Then shall the Priest (or the Bishop, being present) stand up, and turning himself to the people, pronounce this Absolution.

ALMIGHTY God, our heavenly Father, who of his great mercy hath promised forgiveness of sins to all them that with hearty repentance and true faith turn unto him: Have mercy upon you; pardon and deliver you from all your sins; confirm and strengthen you in all goodness; and bring you to everlasting life; through Jesus Christ our Lord. *Amen.*

The foregoing form of Invitation, Confession, and Absolution shall be said on Sundays: but otherwise the following forms may be said at the discretion of the Priest.

DRAW near with faith, and take this Holy Sacrament to your comfort; and make your humble confession to Almighty God, meekly kneeling upon your knees.

Then shall be said by the Minister and people together, kneeling;

WE confess to God Almighty, the Father, the Son, and the Holy Ghost, that we have sinned in thought, word, and deed, through our own grievous fault. Wherefore we pray God to have mercy upon us.

And the Priest (or the Bishop, being present) standing up and turning himself to the people shall say:

ALMIGHTY God have mercy upon you, forgive you all your sins, and deliver you from all evil, confirm and strengthen you in all goodness, and bring you to life everlasting; through Jesus Christ our Lord. *Amen.*

¶ *Then shall the Priest say,*

Hear what comfortable words our Saviour Christ saith unto all that truly turn to him.

COME unto me all that travail and are heavy laden, and I will refresh you. *St. Matthew* 11. 28.

So God loved the world, that he gave his only-begotten Son, to the end that all that believe in him should not perish, but have everlasting life. *St. John* 3. 16.

Hear also what Saint Paul saith.

This is a true saying, and worthy of all men to be received, That Christ Jesus came into the world to save sinners.

1 *Timothy* 1. 15.

Hear also what Saint John saith.

If any man sin, we have an Advocate with the Father, Jesus Christ the righteous; and he is the propitiation for our sins. 1 *St. John* 2. 1.

Then shall the Priest, kneeling down at the Lord's Table, say in the name of all them that shall receive the Holy Communion,

Let us pray.

WE do not presume to come to this thy Table, O merciful Lord, trusting in our own righteousness, but in thy manifold and great mercies. We are not worthy so much as to gather up the crumbs under thy Table. But thou art the same Lord, whose property is always to have mercy: Grant us therefore, gracious Lord, so to eat the Flesh of thy dear Son Jesus Christ, and to drink his Blood, that our sinful bodies may be made clean by his Body, and our souls washed through his most precious Blood, and that we may evermore dwell in him, and he in us. *Amen.*

When the Priest, standing before the Holy Table, hath so ordered the Bread and Wine, that he may with the more readiness and decency break the Bread before the people, and take the Cup into his hands, he shall begin the Consecration, as followeth.

THE CONSECRATION

Turning himself to the people he shall say,

The Lord be with you;

Answer. And with thy spirit.

Priest. Lift up your hearts;

Answer. We lift them up unto the Lord.

Priest. Let us give thanks unto our Lord God;

Answer. It is meet and right so to do.

Then shall the Priest turn to the Lord's Table, and say,

IT is very meet, right, and our bounden duty, that we should at all times, and in all places, give thanks unto thee, O Lord, Holy Father, Almighty, Everlasting God.

Here shall follow the Proper Preface, according to the time, if there be any specially appointed, or else immediately shall follow,

THEREFORE with angels and archangels and with all the company of heaven, we laud and magnify thy glorious name; evermore praising thee, and saying,

HOLY, holy, holy, Lord God of hosts, heaven and earth are full of thy glory. Glory be to thee, O Lord most High. Amen.

Then shall the Priest continue thus.

ALL glory be to thee, Almighty God, our heavenly Father, for that thou of thy tender mercy didst give thine only Son Jesus Christ to suffer death upon the Cross for our redemption; who made there (by his one oblation of himself once offered) a full, perfect, and sufficient sacrifice, oblation, and satisfaction for the sins of the whole world; and did institute, and in his Holy Gospel command us to continue, a perpetual memory of that his precious death until his coming again;

Who, in the same night that he was betrayed, *a*took Bread; and when he had given thanks, *b*he brake it, and gave it to his disciples, saying, Take, eat, *c*this is my Body which is given for you; Do this in remembrance of me. Likewise after supper he *d*took the Cup; and when he had given thanks, he gave it to them, saying, Drink ye all of this; for this *e*is my Blood of the New Covenant, which is shed for you and for many for the remission of sins; Do this, as oft as ye shall drink it, in remembrance of me.

a Here the Priest is to take the Paten into his hands:

b And here to break the Bread:

c And here to lay his hand upon all the Bread.

d Here he is to take the Cup into his hand:

e And here to lay his hand upon every vessel (be it Chalice or Flagon) in which there is any Wine to be consecrated.

Wherefore, O Lord and heavenly Father, we thy humble servants, having in remembrance the precious death and passion of thy dear Son, his mighty resurrection and glorious ascension, according to his holy institution, do celebrate, and set forth before thy Divine Majesty with these thy holy gifts, the memorial which he hath willed us to make, rendering unto thee most hearty thanks for the innumerable benefits which he hath procured unto us.

Hear us, O merciful Father, we most humbly beseech thee, and with thy Holy and Life-giving Spirit vouchsafe to bless and sanctify both us and these thy gifts of Bread and Wine, that they may be unto us the Body and Blood of thy Son, our Saviour, Jesus Christ, to the end that we, receiving the same, may be strengthened and refreshed both in body and soul.

And we entirely desire thy fatherly goodness mercifully to accept this our sacrifice of praise and thanksgiving; most humbly beseeching thee to grant, that by the merits and death of thy Son Jesus Christ, and through faith in his blood, we and all thy whole Church may obtain remission of our sins, and all other benefits of his passion.

And here we offer and present unto thee, O Lord, ourselves, our souls and bodies, to be a reasonable, holy, and living sacrifice unto thee: humbly beseeching thee, that all we, who are partakers of this Holy Communion, may be fulfilled with thy grace and heavenly benediction.

And although we be unworthy, through our manifold sins, to offer unto thee any sacrifice, yet we beseech thee to accept this our bounden duty and service; not weighing our merits, but pardoning our offences;

Through Jesus Christ our Lord, by whom, and with whom, in the unity of the Holy Ghost, all honour and glory be unto thee, O Father Almighty, world without end.

And all the people shall answer Amen.

Here shall the people join with the Priest in the Lord's Prayer, the Priest first saying,

As our Saviour Christ hath commanded and taught us, we are bold to say,

OUR Father, which art in heaven, Hallowed be thy name; Thy kingdom come; Thy will be done; In earth as it is in heaven. Give us this day our daily bread. And forgive us our trespasses, As we forgive them that trespass against us. And lead us not into temptation; But deliver us from evil: For thine is the kingdom, The power, and the glory, For ever and ever. Amen.

Then may the Priest say:

The peace of God be alway with you;
Answer. And with thy spirit.

THE COMMUNION OF THE PRIEST AND PEOPLE

Then shall the Priest first receive the Communion in both kinds himself, and then proceed to deliver the same to the Bishops, Priests, and Deacons, in like manner, (if any be present,) and after that to the people also in order, into their hands, all meekly kneeling. And, when he delivereth the Bread to any one, he shall say,

THE Body of our Lord Jesus Christ, which was given for thee, preserve thy body and soul unto everlasting life. Take and eat this in remembrance that Christ died for thee, and feed on him in thy heart by faith with thanksgiving.

And the Minister that delivereth the Cup to any one shall say,

THE Blood of our Lord Jesus Christ, which was shed for thee, preserve thy body and soul unto everlasting life. Drink this in remembrance that Christ's Blood was shed for thee, and be thankful.

When occasion requires, the Minister may, instead of saying all the above Words of Administration to each communicant, say first in an audible voice to the whole number of them that come to receive the Holy Communion,

DRAW near and receive the Body of our Lord Jesus Christ which was given for you, and his Blood which was shed for you. Take this in remembrance that Christ died for you, and feed on him in your hearts by faith with thanksgiving.

And then in delivering the Bread to each communicant he shall say, either, The Body of our Lord Jesus Christ, which was given for thee, preserve thy body and soul unto everlasting life, *or,* Take and eat this in remembrance that Christ died for thee, and feed on him in thy heart by faith with thanksgiving. *And in delivering the Cup to each communicant he shall say, either,* The Blood of our Lord Jesus Christ, which was shed for thee, preserve thy body and soul unto everlasting life, *or,* Drink this in remembrance that Christ's Blood was shed for thee, and be thankful.

Or else, when occasion requires, the Minister may say the whole form of words once to each row of communicants, or to a convenient number within each row, instead of saying them to each communicant severally.

When all have communicated, the Priest shall return to the Lord's Table, and reverently place upon it what remaineth of the consecrated Elements, covering the same with a fair linen cloth.

THE THANKSGIVING

Then shall the Priest give thanks to God in the name of all them that have communicated, turning him first to the people, and saying,

Having now by faith received the precious Body and Blood of Christ, let us give thanks unto our Lord God.

ALMIGHTY and everliving God, we most heartily thank thee, for that thou dost vouchsafe to feed us, who have duly received these holy mysteries, with the spiritual food of the most precious Body and Blood of thy Son our Saviour

Jesus Christ; and dost assure us thereby of thy favour and goodness towards us; and that we are very members incorporate in the mystical body of thy Son, which is the blessed company of all faithful people; and are also heirs through hope of thy everlasting kingdom, by the merits of the most precious death and passion of thy dear Son. And we most humbly beseech thee, O heavenly Father, so to assist us with thy grace, that we may continue in that holy fellowship, and do all such good works as thou hast prepared for us to walk in; through Jesus Christ our Lord, to whom, with thee and the Holy Ghost, be all honour and glory, world without end. *Amen.*

Then shall the Priest with the people say or sing,

GLORY be to God on high, and in earth peace, good will towards men. We praise thee, we bless thee, we worship thee, we glorify thee, we give thanks to thee for thy great glory, O Lord God, heavenly King, God the Father Almighty.

O Lord, the only-begotten Son Jesu Christ; O Lord God, Lamb of God, Son of the Father, that takest away the sins of the world, have mercy upon us. Thou that takest away the sins of the world, have mercy upon us. Thou that takest away the sins of the world, receive our prayer. Thou that sittest at the right hand of God the Father, have mercy upon us.

For thou only art holy; thou only art the Lord; thou only, O Christ, with the Holy Ghost, art most high in the glory of God the Father. Amen.

At the discretion of the Minister, this Hymn may be omitted on any day not being a Sunday or a Holy-day.

Then the Priest (or the Bishop if he be present), turning to the people, shall let them depart with this Blessing.

THE peace of God, which passeth all understanding, keep your hearts and minds in the knowledge and love of God, and of his Son Jesus Christ our Lord: and the blessing of God Almighty, the Father, the Son, and the Holy Ghost, be amongst you and remain with you always. *Amen.*

¶ *If any of the consecrated Bread and Wine remain, apart from that which may be reserved for the Communion of the sick, as is provided in the Alternative Order for the Communion of the Sick,[1] it shall not be carried out of the church; but the Priest, and such other of the communicants as he shall call unto him, shall, immediately after the Blessing, reverently eat and drink the same.*

¶ *Upon the Sundays and other Holy-days, if there be no Communion, shall be said all that is appointed at the Communion until the end of the Intercession, followed by one or more Collects contained in this Book or sanctioned by the Bishop, and the Service shall be concluded with the Blessing.*

¶ *And whenever this Service is used, Collects, contained in this Book, or sanctioned by the Bishop, may be said after the Intercession, or before the Blessing.*

¶ PROPER PREFACES

Upon Christmas Day *and until the* Epiphany.

BECAUSE thou didst give Jesus Christ thine only Son to be born as at this time for us: Who, by the operation of the Holy Ghost, was made very man of the substance of the Virgin Mary his mother: And that without spot of sin, to make us clean from all sin. Therefore with Angels, *&c.*

Upon the Epiphany *and seven days after*.

THROUGH Jesus Christ our Lord: Who in substance of our mortal flesh manifested forth his glory: That he might bring all men out of darkness into his own marvellous light. Therefore with Angels, *&c.*

Upon the Thursday before Easter.

THROUGH Jesus Christ our Lord: Who having loved his own that were in the world loved them unto the end: And on the night before he suffered, sitting at meat with his disciples, did institute these holy mysteries: That we, redeemed by his death and quickened by his resurrection, might be partakers of his divine nature. Therefore with Angels, *&c.*

Upon Easter Day *and until* Ascension Day.

BUT chiefly are we bound to praise thee for the glorious Resurrection of thy Son Jesus Christ our Lord: For he is the very Paschal Lamb, which was offered for us, and hath

[1] See p. 52.

45

taken away the sin of the world; Who by his death hath destroyed death, and by his rising to life again hath restored to us everlasting life. Therefore with Angels, &c.

Upon Ascension Day *and until* Whitsunday.

THROUGH thy most dearly beloved Son Jesus Christ our Lord: Who after his most glorious Resurrection manifestly appeared to all his Apostles: And in their sight ascended up into heaven to prepare a place for us; That where he is, thither we might also ascend, and reign with him in glory. Therefore with Angels, &c.

Upon Whitsunday *and six days after.*

THROUGH Jesus Christ our Lord: Who after that he had ascended up far above all the heavens, and was set down at the right hand of thy Majesty: Did as at this time pour forth upon the Universal Church thy Holy and Life-giving Spirit: That through his glorious power the joy of the everlasting gospel might go forth into all the world: Whereby we have been brought out of darkness and error into the clear light and true knowledge of thee, and of thy Son our Saviour Jesus Christ. Therefore with Angels, &c.

Upon the Feast of Trinity *only.*

WHO with thine only-begotten Son and the Holy Ghost art one God, one Lord, in Trinity of Persons and in Unity of Substance: For that which we believe of thy glory, O Father, the same we believe of thy Son and of the Holy Ghost, without any difference or inequality. Therefore with Angels, &c.

Upon the Feasts of the Purification *and the* Annunciation.

BECAUSE thou didst give Jesus Christ thine only Son to be born for our salvation: Who by the operation of the Holy Ghost, was made very man of the substance of the Virgin Mary his mother: And that without spot of sin to make us clean from all sin. Therefore with Angels, &c.

46

Upon the Feast of the Transfiguration.

BECAUSE the divine glory of the Incarnate Word shone forth upon the Holy Mount before the chosen witnesses of his majesty: And thine own voice from heaven proclaimed thy beloved Son. Therefore with Angels, *&c.*

Upon All Saints' Day *and the Feasts of Apostles, Evangelists, and* St. John Baptist's Nativity, *except when the Proper Preface of any Principal Feast is appointed.*

WHO in the righteousness of thy Saints hast given us an ensample of godly living, and in their blessedness a glorious pledge of the hope of our calling: That, being compassed about with so great a cloud of witnesses, we may run with patience the race that is set before us: And with them receive the crown of glory that fadeth not away. Therefore with Angels, *&c.*

A Preface which may be used upon the Consecration *of a church, or upon the Feast of its* Dedication.

WHO, though the heaven of heavens cannot contain thee and thy glory is in all the world: Dost deign to hallow places for thy worship, and in them dost pour forth gifts of grace upon thy faithful people. Therefore with Angels, *&c.*

A Preface which may be used upon any Sunday in the year for which no other Proper Preface is appointed.

THROUGH Jesus Christ our Lord; for he is the true High Priest, who hath washed us from our sins, and hath made us to be a kingdom and priests unto thee our God and Father. Therefore with Angels, *&c.*

¶ AN ANTHEM

Which may be said or sung immediately after the words, Glory be to thee, O Lord most high. Amen.

BLESSED is he that cometh in the name of the Lord: Hosanna in the highest.

¶ THE ORDER FOR A SECOND CONSECRATION

If the consecrated Bread and Wine be all spent before all have communicated, the Priest is to consecrate more, according to the form before prescribed, proceeding as follows.

If there be need to consecrate Bread only, he shall first say;

OUR Saviour Christ, in the same night that he was betrayed, took Bread; and when he had given thanks, he brake it, and gave it to his disciples, saying, Take, eat, this is my Body which is given for you; Do this in remembrance of me.

Or if to consecrate Wine only, he shall first say;

LIKEWISE after supper our Saviour took the Cup; and when he had given thanks, he gave it to them, saying, Drink ye all of this; for this is my Blood of the New Covenant, which is shed for you and for many for the remission of sins; Do this, as oft as ye shall drink it, in remembrance of me.

Or if to consecrate both Bread and Wine, he shall first say both of the foregoing;

And thereafter in every case he shall add;

HEAR us, O merciful Father, we most humbly beseech thee, and with thy Holy and Life-giving Spirit vouchsafe to bless and sanctify both us and this (these) thy gift(s) of *Bread* (*and*) *Wine*, that it (they) may be unto us the *Body* (*and*) *Blood* of thy Son, our Saviour, Jesus Christ, to the end that we, receiving the same, may be strengthened and refreshed both in body and soul. *Amen.*

¶ THE EXHORTATIONS

To be used when the Minister giveth warning for the celebration of the Holy Communion.

DEARLY beloved, on —— I purpose, through God's assistance, to administer to all such as shall be religiously and devoutly disposed the most comfortable Sacrament of the Body and Blood of Christ; to be by them received in remembrance of his meritorious Cross and Passion; whereby alone we obtain remission of our sins, and are made partakers of the kingdom of heaven.

Wherefore it is our duty to render most humble and hearty thanks to Almighty God our heavenly Father, for that he hath given his Son our Saviour Jesus Christ, not only to die for us, but also to be our spiritual food and sustenance in that Holy Sacrament.

Which being so divine and comfortable a thing to them who receive it worthily, and so dangerous to them that will presume to receive it unworthily; my duty is to exhort you in the mean season to consider the dignity of that holy mystery, and the great peril of the unworthy receiving thereof; and so to search and examine your own consciences, (and that not lightly, and after the manner of dissemblers with God; but so) that ye may come holy and clean to such a heavenly Feast, in the marriage-garment required by God in Holy Scripture, and be received as worthy partakers of that Holy Table.

The way and means thereto is; First, to examine your lives and conversations by the rule of God's commandments; and whereinsoever ye shall perceive yourselves to have offended, either by will, word, or deed, there to bewail your own sinfulness, and to confess yourselves to Almighty God, with full purpose of amendment of life.

And if ye shall perceive your offences to be such as are not only against God, but also against your neighbours; then ye shall reconcile yourselves unto them; being ready to make restitution and satisfaction, according to the uttermost of your powers, for all injuries and wrongs done by you to any other; and being likewise ready to forgive others that have offended you, as ye would have forgiveness of your offences at God's hand: for otherwise the receiving of the Holy Communion doth nothing else but increase your guilt.

Therefore if any of you be a blasphemer of God, an hinderer or slanderer of his Word, an adulterer, or be in malice, or envy, or in any other grievous crime, repent you of your sins, or else come not to that Holy Table.

E

49

And because it is requisite, that no man should come to the Holy Communion, but with a full trust in God's mercy, and with a quiet conscience; therefore if there be any of you, who by this means cannot quiet his own conscience herein, but requireth further comfort or counsel, let him come to me, or to some other discreet and learned Minister of God's Word, and open his grief; that by the ministry of God's holy Word he may receive the benefit of absolution, together with ghostly counsel and advice, to the quieting of his conscience, and avoiding of all scruple and doubtfulness.

Or, in case he shall see the people negligent to come to the Holy Communion, instead of the former, he may use this Exhortation.

DEARLY beloved brethren, on —— I intend, by God's grace, to celebrate the Lord's Supper: unto which, in God's behalf, I bid you all that are here present; and beseech you, for the Lord Jesus Christ's sake, that ye will not refuse to come thereto, being so lovingly called and bidden by God himself.

Ye know how grievous and unkind a thing it is, when a man hath prepared a rich feast, decked his table with all kind of provision, so that there lacketh nothing but the guests to sit down; and yet they who are called (without any cause) most unthankfully refuse to come. Which of you in such a case would not be moved? Who would not think a great injury and wrong done unto him? Wherefore, most dearly beloved in Christ, take ye good heed, lest ye, withdrawing yourselves from this Holy Supper, provoke God's indignation against you. It is an easy matter for a man to say, I will not communicate, because I am otherwise hindered with worldly business. But such excuses are not so easily accepted and allowed before God. If any man say, I am a grievous sinner, and therefore am afraid to come: wherefore then do ye not repent and amend? When God calleth you, are ye not ashamed to say ye will not come? When ye should return to God, will ye excuse yourselves, and say ye are not ready? Consider earnestly with yourselves how little such feigned excuses will avail before God.

They that refused the feast in the Gospel, because they had bought a farm, or would try their yokes of oxen, or because they were married, were not so excused, but counted unworthy of the heavenly feast.

I, for my part, shall be ready; and, according to mine office, I bid you in the name of God, I call you in Christ's behalf, I exhort you, as ye love your own salvation, that ye will be partakers of this Holy Communion. And as the Son of God did vouchsafe to yield up his soul by death upon the Cross for your salvation; so it is your duty to receive the Communion in remembrance of the sacrifice of his death, as he himself hath commanded: which if ye shall neglect to do, consider with yourselves how great injury ye do unto God, and how sore punishment hangeth over your heads for the same; when ye wilfully abstain from the Lord's Table, and separate from your brethren, who come to feed on the banquet of that most heavenly food.

These things if ye earnestly consider, ye will by God's grace return to a better mind: for the obtaining whereof we shall not cease to make our humble petitions unto Almighty God our heavenly Father.

¶ Whereas it is ordained in this Office for the Administration of the Lord's Supper, that the communicants should receive the same kneeling; (which order is well meant, for a signification of our humble and grateful acknowledgement of the benefits of Christ therein given to all worthy receivers, and for the avoiding of such profanation and disorder in the Holy Communion, as might otherwise ensue;) yet, lest the same kneeling should by any persons, either out of ignorance and infirmity, or out of malice and obstinacy, be misconstrued and depraved; It is hereby declared, That thereby no adoration is intended, or ought to be done, either unto the Sacramental Bread or Wine there bodily received, or unto any Corporal Presence of Christ's natural Flesh and Blood. For the Sacramental Bread and Wine remain still in their very natural substances, and therefore may not be adored; (for that were idolatry, to be abhorred of all faithful Christians;) and the natural Body and Blood of our Saviour Christ are in Heaven, and not here; it being against the truth of Christ's natural Body to be at one time in more places than one.

The 'Alternative Order for the Communion of the Sick' to which the rubric on p. 45 refers, is as follows:

¶ *When the Holy Communion cannot reverently or without grave difficulty be celebrated in private, and also when there are several sick persons in the Parish desirous to receive the Communion on the same day, it shall be lawful for the Priest (with the consent of the sick person or persons), on any day when there is a celebration of the Holy Communion in the church, to set apart at the open Communion so much of the consecrated Bread and Wine as shall serve the sick person (or persons), and so many as shall communicate with him (if there be any). And, the open Communion ended, he shall, on the same day and with as little delay as may be, go and minister the same.*

¶ *If the Bishop is satisfied that in connexion with hospitals, or in time of common sickness, or in the special circumstances of any particular Parish, the provisions of the preceding rubric are not sufficient, and that there is need of further provision in order that sick and dying persons may not lack the benefit of the most comfortable Sacrament of the Body and Blood of Christ, he may to that end give his licence to the Priest, to reserve at the open Communion so much of the consecrated Bread and Wine as is needed for the purpose. Whenever such licence is granted or refused, the Minister, or the people as represented in the Parochial Church Council, may refer the question to the Archbishop and Bishops of the Province.*

¶ *The consecrated Bread and Wine set apart under either of the two preceding rubrics shall be reserved only for the Communion of the Sick, shall be administered in both kinds, and shall be used for no other purpose whatever. There shall be no service or ceremony in connexion with the Sacrament so reserved, nor shall it be exposed or removed except in order to be received in Communion, or otherwise reverently consumed.*

¶ *The consecrated Bread and Wine thus set apart shall be reserved in an aumbry or safe. The aumbry shall (according as the Bishop shall direct) be set in the North or South wall of the sanctuary of the church or of any chapel thereof, or, if need be, in the wall of some other part of the church approved by the Bishop, provided that it shall not be immediately behind or above a Holy Table. The door of the aumbry shall be kept locked, and opened only when it is necessary to move or replace the consecrated Elements for the purposes of Communion or renewal. The consecrated Bread and Wine shall be renewed at least once a week.*

¶ *When the consecrated Bread and Wine are taken from the church to the sick person, before the Priest administers the Holy Sacrament, he shall use at least the parts of the appointed Order of Holy Communion here named: the General Confession and Absolution, (which may be in the shorter form), and the Prayer, We do not presume, &c., except when extreme sickness shall otherwise require: and after the delivery of the Sacrament of Christ's Body and Blood with the appointed words, he shall say the Lord's Prayer and the Blessing.*

¶ *Immediately after the ministration to the sick person, or to the last of the sick persons (if there be more than one), any of the consecrated Elements that remain shall be reverently consumed at the place of such ministration, or, if the reservation be under the second rubric of the Order, may be taken back to the church.*

¶ *When it is desirable to administer both kinds together, the words of administration shall be said thus:*

THE Body of our Lord Jesus Christ, which was given for thee, and his Blood, which was shed for thee, preserve thy body and soul unto everlasting life. Take this in remembrance that Christ died for thee, and feed on him in thy heart by faith with thanksgiving.

¶ *Note, that the same Form shall be used, with the permission of the Bishop, when it is deemed necessary, through grave danger of infection, to administer both kinds together to certain communicants at the open Communion.*

THE SCOTTISH LITURGY
(1929)

GENERAL RUBRICS

APPLICABLE TO BOTH THE AUTHORIZED OFFICES OF

HOLY COMMUNION

It is desirable that so many as intend to be partakers of the Holy Communion should signify their names to the Priest.

The Priest shall sing or say the Service in a distinct and audible voice.

Upon the Sundays and other Holy-days (if there be no Communion) may be said all that is appointed at the Communion until the end of the Sentences appointed for the Offertory, together with one or more of the Collects in the Appendix, concluding with the Blessing.

And in Cathedral and Collegiate Churches, and Colleges, where there are many Priests and Deacons, they shall all receive the Communion with the Priest every Sunday at the least, except they have a reasonable cause to the contrary.

It is desirable that the Bread for the Holy Communion shall be the best and purest wheat bread, whether loaf or wafer, that conveniently may be gotten.

It is customary to mix a little pure water with the Wine in the Eucharistic Cup.

According to long-existing custom in the Scottish Church, the Presbyter may reserve so much of the consecrated Gifts as may be required for the Communion of the Sick and others who could not be present at the celebration in church. All that remaineth of the Holy Sacrament, and is not so required, the Presbyter and such other of the communicants as he shall then call unto him shall, after the Blessing, reverently eat and drink.

It is the duty of every confirmed member of the Church to receive the Holy Sacrament with frequency, and especially to receive it at Easter and at the other Great Festivals of the Church.

It is hereby declared that it is the duty of the Minister to use and observe the Order for Holy Communion without diminishing therefrom or adding thereto. The Order here provided shall not be supplemented by additional prayers save so far as may be ordered or permitted by the Bishop.

At every celebration of the Holy Communion reasonable opportunity to communicate shall be given to the people who wish to do so.

THE SCOTTISH LITURGY

FOR THE CELEBRATION OF THE HOLY EUCHARIST
AND ADMINISTRATION OF HOLY COMMUNION

COMMONLY CALLED

THE SCOTTISH COMMUNION OFFICE

THE INTRODUCTION

The Holy Table, having at the Communion time a fair white linen cloth upon it, with other decent furniture meet for the High Mysteries there to be celebrated, shall stand at the uppermost part of the chancel or church. And the Presbyter, standing at the Holy Table, shall say the Collect following for due preparation, the people kneeling.

ALMIGHTY God, unto whom all hearts be open, all desires known, and from whom no secrets are hid: Cleanse the thoughts of our hearts by the inspiration of thy Holy Spirit, that we may perfectly love thee, and worthily magnify thy holy Name; through Christ our Lord. *Amen.*

Then shall the Presbyter, turning to the people, rehearse distinctly all the Ten Commandments: the people all the while kneeling, and asking God mercy for the transgression of every duty therein, according to the letter or to the spiritual import of each Commandment, and grace to keep the same for the time to come. The Ten Commandments may be rehearsed in the short form by stopping at the asterisks.

GOD spake these words and said; I am the Lord thy God: Thou shalt have none other gods but me.

People. Lord, have mercy upon us, and incline our hearts to keep this law.

Presbyter. Thou shalt not make to thyself any graven image, nor the likeness of any thing that is in heaven above, or in the earth beneath, or in the water under the earth. Thou shalt not bow down to them, nor worship them.* For I the Lord thy God am a jealous God, and visit the sins of the fathers upon the children unto the third and fourth

56

generation of them that hate me, and shew mercy unto thousands in them that love me, and keep my commandments.

People. Lord, have mercy upon us, and incline our hearts to keep this law.

Presbyter. Thou shalt not take the Name of the Lord thy God in vain.* For the Lord will not hold him guiltless, that taketh his Name in vain.

People. Lord, have mercy upon us, and incline our hearts to keep this law.

Presbyter. Remember that thou keep holy the sabbath-day. Six days shalt thou labour, and do all that thou hast to do;* but the seventh day is the sabbath of the Lord thy God. In it thou shalt do no manner of work, thou, and thy son, and thy daughter, thy man-servant, and thy maid-servant, thy cattle, and the stranger that is within thy gates. For in six days the Lord made heaven and earth, the sea, and all that in them is, and rested the seventh day: wherefore the Lord blessed the seventh day, and hallowed it.

People. Lord, have mercy upon us, and incline our hearts to keep this law.

Presbyter. Honour thy father and thy mother;* that thy days may be long in the land which the Lord thy God giveth thee.

People. Lord, have mercy upon us, and incline our hearts to keep this law.

Presbyter. Thou shalt do no murder.

People. Lord, have mercy upon us, and incline our hearts to keep this law.

Presbyter. Thou shalt not commit adultery.

People. Lord, have mercy upon us, and incline our hearts to keep this law.

Presbyter. Thou shalt not steal.

People. Lord, have mercy upon us, and incline our hearts to keep this law.

57

Presbyter. Thou shalt not bear false witness against thy neighbour.

People. Lord, have mercy upon us, and incline our hearts to keep this law.

Presbyter. Thou shalt not covet* thy neighbour's house, thou shalt not covet thy neighbour's wife, nor his servant, nor his maid, nor his ox, nor his ass, nor any thing that is his.

People. Lord, have mercy upon us, and write all these thy laws in our hearts, we beseech thee.

Or he may rehearse, instead of the Ten Commandments, the Summary of the Law as followeth:

OUR Lord Jesus Christ said: Hear, O Israel, the Lord our God is one Lord: and thou shalt love the Lord thy God with all thy heart, and with all thy soul, and with all thy mind, and with all thy strength: This is the first commandment. And the second is like, namely this, Thou shalt love thy neighbour as thyself: there is none other commandment greater than these.

On these two commandments hang all the Law and the Prophets.

People. Lord, have mercy upon us, and write these thy laws in our hearts, we beseech thee.

Or else, instead of, or in addition to, the Ten Commandments or the Summary of the Law, may be sung or said as followeth:

LORD, have mercy upon us.
Christ, have mercy upon us.
Lord, have mercy upon us.

Then shall the Presbyter say,

THE Lord be with you;
Answer. And with thy spirit.

Then shall be said the Collect or Collects, the Presbyter standing as before and first saying,

Let us pray.

THE MINISTRY OF THE WORD

Then the Presbyter, or some other Presbyter or Deacon, turning to the people, shall read the Epistle or Lesson, saying, The Epistle [or The Lesson] is written in the —— chapter of —— beginning at the —— verse. And, the Epistle or Lesson ended, he shall say, Here endeth the Epistle [or Lesson]. Then shall the Presbyter, or some other Presbyter or Deacon, turning to the people, read the Gospel, saying, The Holy Gospel is written in the —— chapter of the Gospel according to ——, beginning at the —— verse; and the people, all standing up, shall devoutly sing or say,

Glory be to thee, O Lord.

And, the Gospel ended, the people shall in like manner sing or say,

Thanks be to thee, O Lord, for this thy glorious Gospel.

Then shall be sung or said this Creed following, the people still reverently standing.

I BELIEVE in one God the Father Almighty, Maker of heaven and earth, And of all things visible and invisible: And in one Lord Jesus Christ, the only-begotten Son of God, Begotten of his Father before all worlds, God of God, Light of Light, Very God of Very God, Begotten, not made, Being of one substance with the Father, By whom all things were made: Who for us men, and for our salvation came down from heaven, And was incarnate by the Holy Ghost of the Virgin Mary, And was made man, And was crucified also for us under Pontius Pilate. He suffered and was buried, And the third day he rose again according to the Scriptures, And ascended into heaven, And sitteth on the right hand of the Father. And he shall come again with glory to judge both the quick and the dead: Whose kingdom shall have no end.

And I believe in the Holy Ghost, The Lord, The Giver of life, Who proceedeth from the Father and the Son, Who with the Father and the Son together is worshipped and glorified, Who spake by the Prophets. And I believe one Holy Catholic and Apostolic Church. I acknowledge one Baptism for the remission of sins. And I look for the Resurrection of the dead, And the Life of the world to come. Amen.

Then the Presbyter shall declare unto the people what Holy-days or Fasting-days are to be observed in the week. And also (if occasion be) notice shall be given of the Holy Communion; Banns of Matrimony may be published; and, subject to the authority of the Bishop, other notices may be read.

If there be a Sermon, it followeth here.

When the Presbyter giveth warning of the Holy Communion he may, at his discretion, use the first or the second of the Exhortations appended on pp. 81–84.

The Exhortation appended on p. 84 may be used at the discretion of the Presbyter before the Offertory, the people standing.

The Presbyter may here bid special prayers and thanksgivings.

THE OFFERTORY

Then, the people standing until after the Sanctus, the Presbyter, or Deacon, shall say,

LET us present our offerings to the Lord with reverence and godly fear.

Then the Presbyter shall begin the Offertory, saying one or more of these Sentences following, as he thinketh most convenient.

I WILL offer in his dwelling an oblation with great gladness; I will sing and speak praises unto the Lord.
Psalm 27. 7.

Offer unto God thanksgiving, and pay thy vows unto the most Highest.
Psalm 50. 14.

Give unto the Lord the glory due unto his Name: bring an offering, and come into his courts.
Psalm 96. 8.

I will offer to thee the sacrifice of thanksgiving, and will call upon the Name of the Lord; I will pay my vows unto the Lord in the sight of all his people.
Psalm 116. 15, 16.

Not every one that saith unto me, Lord, Lord, shall enter into the kingdom of heaven: but he that doeth the will of my Father which is in heaven.
St. Matthew 7. 21.

Remember the words of the Lord Jesus, how he said, It is more blessed to give than to receive.
Acts 20. 35.

As we have opportunity, let us do good unto all men; especially unto them who are of the household of faith.

Galatians 6. 10.

To do good and to communicate forget not; for with such sacrifices God is well-pleased. *Hebrews* 13. 16.

While the Presbyter distinctly pronounceth one or more of these Sentences for the Offertory, the Deacon, or (if no such be present) some other fit person, shall receive the devotions of the people there present, in a bason provided for that purpose. And when all have offered, he shall reverently bring the said bason, with the offerings therein, and deliver it to the Presbyter; who shall humbly present it before the Lord, and set it upon the Holy Table.

And the Presbyter shall then offer up, and place the bread and wine prepared for the Sacrament upon the Lord's Table; and shall say,

BLESSED be thou, O Lord God, for ever and ever. Thine, O Lord, is the greatness, and the glory, and the victory, and the majesty: for all that is in the heaven and in the earth is thine: thine is the kingdom, O Lord, and thou art exalted as head above all: both riches and honour come of thee, and of thine own do we give unto thee. *Amen.*

THE CONSECRATION

Then shall the Presbyter say,

THE Lord be with you;
   Answer. And with thy spirit.

Presbyter. Lift up your hearts;
Answer. We lift them up unto the Lord.

Presbyter. Let us give thanks unto our Lord God;
Answer. It is meet and right so to do.

Presbyter.

IT is very meet, right, and our bounden duty, that we should at all times, and in all places, give thanks unto thee, O Lord, Holy Father, Almighty, Everlasting God.

Here shall follow the Proper Preface, according to the time, if there be any especially appointed (see pp. 73–79); or else immediately shall follow,

61

THEREFORE with Angels and Archangels, and with all the company of heaven, we laud and magnify thy glorious Name; evermore praising thee and saying:

HOLY, holy, holy, Lord God of hosts, heaven and earth are full of thy glory. Glory be to thee, O Lord most high. Amen. *Presbyter and People.*

Here may be sung or said:

BLESSED is he that cometh in the Name of the Lord. Hosanna in the highest.

When this is sung or said, Amen *shall be omitted after the Sanctus.*

Then the Presbyter, standing at such a part of the Holy Table as he may with the most ease and decency use both his hands, shall say the Prayer of Consecration, as followeth:

ALL glory and thanksgiving be to thee, Almighty God, our heavenly Father, for that thou of thy tender mercy didst give thine only Son Jesus Christ to suffer death upon the cross for our redemption; who, by his own oblation of himself once offered, made a full, perfect, and sufficient sacrifice, oblation, and satisfaction, for the sins of the whole world; and did institute, and in his holy Gospel command us to continue, a perpetual memorial of that his precious death and sacrifice until his coming again.

For, in the night that he was betrayed, *a*he took bread; and when he had given thanks, *b*he brake it, and gave it to his disciples, saying, Take, eat, *c*this is my Body, which is given for you: Do this in remembrance of me. Likewise after supper *d*he took the cup; and when he had given thanks, he gave it to them, saying, Drink ye all of this, for *e*this is my Blood of the new testament, which is shed for you and for many for the remission of sins: Do this as oft as ye shall drink it in remembrance of me.

a Here the Presbyter is to take the paten in his hands:

b And here to break the bread:

c And here to lay his hands upon all the bread.

d Here he is to take the cup into his hand:

e And here to lay his hand upon every vessel (be it chalice or flagon) in which there is any wine to be consecrated.

Wherefore, O Lord, and heavenly Father, according to the institution of thy dearly beloved Son our Saviour Jesus Christ, we thy humble servants *The Oblation.* do celebrate and make here before thy Divine Majesty, with these thy holy gifts, which we now offer unto thee, the memorial thy Son hath commanded us to make; having in remembrance his blessed passion, and precious death, his mighty resurrection, and glorious ascension; rendering unto thee most hearty thanks for the innumerable benefits procured unto us by the same, and looking for his coming again with power and great glory.

And we thine unworthy servants beseech thee, most merciful Father, to hear us, and to send thy Holy Spirit upon us and upon these thy gifts *The Invocation.* and creatures of bread and wine, that, being blessed and hallowed by his life-giving power, they may become the Body and Blood of thy most dearly beloved Son, to the end that all who shall receive the same may be sanctified both in body and soul, and preserved unto everlasting life.

And we earnestly desire thy fatherly goodness, mercifully to accept this our sacrifice of praise and thanksgiving, most humbly beseeching thee to grant, that by the merits and death of thy Son Jesus Christ, and through faith in his blood, we and all thy whole Church may obtain remission of our sins, and all other benefits of his passion.

And here we humbly offer and present unto thee, O Lord, ourselves, our souls and bodies, to be a reasonable, holy, and living sacrifice unto thee, beseeching thee that all we who shall be partakers of this Holy Communion may worthily receive the most precious Body and Blood of thy Son Jesus Christ, and be fulfilled with thy grace and heavenly benediction, and made one body with him, that he may dwell in us and we in him.

And although we be unworthy, through our manifold sins, to offer unto thee any sacrifice; yet we beseech thee to accept this our bounden duty and service, not weighing our merits, but pardoning our offences, through Jesus Christ our Lord: by whom, and with whom, in the unity of the Holy

Ghost, all honour and glory be unto thee, O Father Almighty, world without end. *Amen.*

Let us pray for the whole state of Christ's Church.

The Presbyter.

ALMIGHTY and Everliving God, who by thy holy Apostle hast taught us to make intercessions and to give thanks for all men: We humbly pray thee most mercifully to receive these our supplications which we offer unto thy Divine Majesty; beseeching thee to inspire continually the universal Church with the spirit of truth, unity, and concord; and grant that all they that do confess thy holy Name may agree in the truth of thy holy word, and live in unity and godly love.

We beseech thee also to save and defend all Kings, Princes, and Governors, and especially thy servant *George* our King, and all who are put in authority under him, that we may be godly and quietly governed.

Give grace, O heavenly Father, to all Bishops, Priests, and Deacons, [and especially to thy servant *N.* our Bishop,] that they may both by their life and doctrine set forth thy true and living word, and rightly and duly administer thy holy Sacraments: and to all thy people give thy heavenly grace, and especially to this Congregation here present, that they may hear and receive thy holy word, truly serving thee in holiness and righteousness all the days of their life.

We most humbly beseech thee of thy goodness, O Lord, to comfort and succour all those who in this transitory life are in trouble, sorrow, need, sickness, or any other adversity.

We commend to thy gracious keeping, O Lord, all thy servants departed this life in thy faith and fear, beseeching thee to grant them everlasting light and peace.

And we yield unto thee most high praise and hearty

thanks, for the wonderful grace and virtue declared in all thy Saints, who have been the choice vessels of thy grace, and the lights of the world in their several generations:[1] beseeching thee to give us grace to follow the example of their stedfastness in thy faith, and obedience to thy holy commandments, that at the day of the general resurrection, we, and all they who are of the mystical body of thy Son, may be set on his right hand, and hear his most joyful voice, Come ye blessed of my Father, inherit the kingdom prepared for you from the foundation of the world.

Grant this, O Father, for Jesus Christ's sake, our only Mediator and Advocate. *Amen.*

Then shall the Presbyter say,

As our Saviour Christ hath commanded and taught us, we are bold to say,

OUR Father which art in heaven, Hallowed be thy Name, Thy kingdom come, Thy will be done, in earth as it is in heaven. Give us this day *Presbyter and People.* our daily bread; And forgive us our trespasses, As we forgive them that trespass against us; And lead us not into temptation, But deliver us from evil. For thine is the kingdom, the power, and the glory, For ever and ever. Amen.

Here the Presbyter shall break the consecrated Bread; and silence may be kept for a brief space.

Then shall the Presbyter say:

THE peace of the Lord be with you all;
Answer. And with thy spirit.
Presbyter. Brethren, let us love one another, for love is of God.

[1] *On feasts of the Blessed Virgin and the Saints for which a Proper Preface is provided, this commemoration may be inserted with the Bishop's consent:* and chiefly in the Blessed Virgin Mary, Mother of thy Son Jesus Christ our Lord and God, and in the Holy Patriarchs, Prophets, Apostles, and Martyrs, beseeching thee to give us grace, &c.

COMMUNION

YE that do truly and earnestly repent you of your sins, and are in love and charity with your neighbours, and intend to lead a new life, following the commandments of God, and walking from henceforth in his holy ways: Draw near with faith, and take this Holy Sacrament to your comfort; and make your humble confession to Almighty God, meekly kneeling upon your knees.

Then shall this general Confession be made by the people, along with the Presbyter; he first kneeling down.

ALMIGHTY God, Father of our Lord Jesus Christ, Maker of all things, Judge of all men: We acknowledge and bewail our manifold sins and wickedness, Which we from time to time most grievously have committed, By thought, word, and deed, Against thy Divine Majesty, Provoking most justly thy wrath and indignation against us. We do earnestly repent, And are heartily sorry for these our misdoings; The remembrance of them is grievous unto us; The burden of them is intolerable. Have mercy upon us, Have mercy upon us, most merciful Father; For thy Son our Lord Jesus Christ's sake, Forgive us all that is past; And grant that we may ever hereafter Serve and please thee In newness of life, To the honour and glory of thy Name; Through Jesus Christ our Lord. Amen.

Then shall the Presbyter, or the Bishop if he be present, stand up, and, turning himself to the people, pronounce the Absolution as followeth:

ALMIGHTY God, our heavenly Father, who of his great mercy hath promised forgiveness of sins to all them who with hearty repentance and true faith turn unto him: Have mercy upon you; pardon and deliver you from all your sins; confirm and strengthen you in all goodness; and bring you to everlasting life; through Jesus Christ our Lord. *Amen.*

Then shall the Presbyter also say,

Hear what comfortable words our Saviour Christ saith
unto all that truly turn to him.

COME unto me all ye that labour and are heavy laden,
and I will give you rest. *St. Matthew* 11. 28.

God so loved the world, that he gave his only-begotten
Son, that whosoever believeth in him should not perish, but
have everlasting life. *St. John* 3. 16.

Hear also what Saint Paul saith.

This is a faithful saying, and worthy of all acceptation,
that Christ Jesus came into the world to save sinners.
1 *Timothy* 1. 15.

Hear also what Saint John saith.

If any man sin, we have an Advocate with the Father,
Jesus Christ the righteous: and he is the propitiation for
our sins. 1 *St. John* 2. 1, 2.

*Then shall the Presbyter, turning him to the Altar, kneel down, and say, in the
name of all of them that shall communicate, this Collect of humble access to the
Holy Communion, as followeth:*

WE do not presume to come to this thy Holy Table, O
merciful Lord, trusting in our own righteousness, but
in thy manifold and great mercies. We are not worthy so
much as to gather up the crumbs under thy Table: but thou
art the same Lord, whose property is always to have mercy.
Grant us therefore, gracious Lord, so to eat the Flesh of thy
dear Son Jesus Christ, and to drink his Blood, that our
sinful bodies may be made clean by his most sacred Body,
and our souls washed through his most precious Blood, and
that we may evermore dwell in him, and he in us. *Amen.*

Here may be sung or said:

O LAMB of God, that takest away the sins of the world:
have mercy upon us.

O Lamb of God, that takest away the sins of the world:
have mercy upon us.

O Lamb of God, that takest away the sins of the world:
grant us thy peace.

Then shall he that celebrateth first receive the Communion in both kinds himself, and next deliver the same to the Bishops, Presbyters, and Deacons (if there be any present), and after to the people in due order, into their hands, all humbly kneeling. And when he receiveth himself or delivereth the Sacrament of the Body of Christ to any other, he shall say,

THE Body of our Lord Jesus Christ, which was given for thee, preserve thy body and soul unto everlasting life.

Here the person receiving shall say,

Amen.

And the Presbyter that receiveth the Cup himself, as likewise the Presbyter or Deacon that delivereth it to any other, shall say,

THE Blood of our Lord Jesus Christ, which was shed for thee, preserve thy body and soul unto everlasting life.

Here the person receiving shall say,

Amen.

If the consecrated Bread or Wine be all spent before all have communicated, the Presbyter is to consecrate more in both kinds, according to the Form appended to this Liturgy.

When all have communicated, he that celebrateth shall go to the Lord's Table, and cover with a fair linen cloth that which remaineth of the consecrated Elements.

THANKSGIVING AFTER COMMUNION

Then the Presbyter or Deacon, turning to the people, shall say,

HAVING now received the precious Body and Blood of Christ, let us give thanks to our Lord God, who hath graciously vouchsafed to admit us to the participation of his Holy Mysteries; and let us beg of him grace to perform our vows, and to persevere in our good resolutions; and that being made holy, we may obtain everlasting life, through the merits of the all-sufficient sacrifice of our Lord and Saviour Jesus Christ.

This Exhortation may be omitted except on Sundays and the Great Festivals.

Then the Presbyter shall say this Collect of thanksgiving as followeth:

ALMIGHTY and Everliving God, we most heartily thank thee, for that thou dost vouchsafe to feed us, who have duly received these Holy Mysteries, with the spiritual food of the most precious Body and Blood of thy Son our Saviour Jesus Christ; and dost assure us thereby of thy favour and goodness towards us, and that we are very members incorporate in the mystical Body of thy Son, which is the blessed company of all faithful people; and are also heirs through hope of thy everlasting kingdom, by the merits of his most precious death and passion. We now most humbly beseech thee, O heavenly Father, so to assist us with thy Holy Spirit, that we may continue in that holy communion and fellowship, and do all such good works as thou hast prepared for us to walk in; through Jesus Christ our Lord, to whom, with thee and the Holy Ghost, be all honour and glory, world without end. *Amen.*

Then shall be sung or said Gloria in excelsis, *by the Presbyter and people as followeth:*

GLORY be to God in the highest, and in earth peace, good will towards men. We praise thee, we bless thee, we worship thee, we glorify thee, we give thanks to thee for thy great glory, O Lord God, heavenly King, God the Father Almighty; and to thee, O God, the only-begotten Son Jesu Christ; and to thee, O God, the Holy Ghost.

O Lord, the only-begotten Son, Jesu Christ; O Lord God, Lamb of God, Son of the Father, who takest away the sins of the world, have mercy upon us. Thou that takest away the sins of the world, receive our prayer. Thou that sittest at the right hand of God the Father, have mercy upon us.

For thou only art holy, thou only art the Lord, thou only, O Christ, with the Holy Ghost, art most high in the glory of God the Father. Amen.

For the Post-Communions see pp. 77–9.

Then the Presbyter, or the Bishop if he be present, shall let them depart with this Blessing.

THE peace of God which passeth all understanding, keep your hearts and minds in the knowledge and love of God, and of his Son Jesus Christ our Lord: And the blessing of God Almighty, the Father, the Son, and the Holy Ghost, be amongst you and remain with you always. *Amen.*

The Creed, the Exhortation Ye that do truly, *the* Comfortable Words, *and the* Gloria in excelsis *may be omitted on Weekdays except on Red Letter Days.*

THE ORDER FOR A SECOND CONSECRATION

IF THE CONSECRATED BREAD OR WINE BE ALL SPENT
BEFORE ALL HAVE COMMUNICATED

The Presbyter shall consecrate more in both kinds, saying:

OUR Lord Jesus Christ, in the night that he was betrayed, *a*took bread; and when he had given thanks, *b*he brake it, and gave it to his disciples, saying, Take, eat, *c*this is my Body, which is given for you: Do this in remembrance of me. Likewise after supper *d*he took the cup; and when he had given thanks, he gave it to them, saying, Drink ye all of this, for *e*this is my Blood of the new testament, which is shed for you and for many for the remission of sins: Do this as oft as ye shall drink it in remembrance of me.

a Here the Presbyter is to take the paten in his hands:

b And here to break the bread:

c And here to lay his hands upon all the bread.

d Here he is to take the cup into his hand:

e And here to lay his hand upon every vessel (be it chalice or flagon) in which there is any wine to be consecrated.

We thine unworthy servants therefore beseech thee, most merciful Father, to hear us, and to send thy Holy Spirit upon us and upon these thy gifts and creatures of bread and wine, that, being blessed and hallowed by his life-giving power, they may become the Body and Blood of thy most dearly beloved Son, to the end that all who shall receive the same may be sanctified both in body and soul, and preserved unto everlasting life.

And the people shall say,

Amen.

[Here follows 'The Order for the Administration of the Lord's Supper or Holy Communion', which corresponds closely with the English rite of 1662 but is set out so as to make the pre-Offertory portion of the service conform to the Scottish Liturgy (save that the recitation of the Ten Commandments is required 'once a month', the Salutation before the Collect of the Day is not present, and the two responses at the Gospel are only permissive). The Creed, therefore, as in the English 1928, contains the words 'The Lord, The Giver of life', and 'one Holy Catholic and Apostolic Church'.

One Offertory Sentence is added (Acts 20. 35), and after the offering of the elements the Priest may say:

THINE, O Lord, is the greatness, and the power, and the glory, and the victory, and the majesty; for all that is in the heaven and in the earth is thine; thine is the kingdom, O Lord, and thou art exalted as head above all. All things come of thee, and of thine own have we given thee.

A rubric before the Prayer for the Church allows the Priest to bid special prayers and thanksgivings.

At the Communion of the People, the Priest at his discretion may use the first half only of each Form of Administration.

After the Prayer of Thanksgiving, there follows the rubric '*Both the prayers* O Lord and heavenly Father *and* Almighty and Ever-living God *may be said in succession at the same service.*'; and after 'Glory be to God on high', a reference is given to the Post Communions on pp. 77–9.

The general rubrics prefixed to the Scottish Liturgy, being applicable to both services, authorize the mixed chalice and reservation for the sick, whichever rite is followed.]

APPENDIX

The following are for use with both the authorized Offices of Holy Communion.

PROPER PREFACES

Advent.

BECAUSE thou hast given salvation unto mankind through the coming of thy well-beloved Son in great humility, and by him wilt make all things new when he shall come again in his glorious majesty to judge the world in righteousness. Therefore with Angels, &c.

Upon Christmas Day, *and until the* Eve of the Epiphany *inclusive.*

BECAUSE thou didst give Jesus Christ thine only Son, to be born *[as on this day] for us; who, by the operation of the Holy Ghost, was made very man, of the substance of the Blessed Virgin Mary his mother, and that without spot of sin, to make us clean from all sin. Therefore with Angels, &c.

* During the days after Christmas say, as at this time.

The Proper Preface for Christmas may be used on all Feasts of the Blessed Virgin Mary not otherwise provided for, but the words as on this day *shall then be omitted.*

Upon The Epiphany, *and seven days after.*

THROUGH Jesus Christ our Lord; who, in substance of our mortal flesh, manifested forth his glory, that he might bring us out of darkness into his own marvellous light. Therefore with Angels, &c.

Upon The Purification.

BECAUSE thy blessed Son Jesus Christ our Lord, born of a woman, born under the Law, was, as on this day, presented in the Temple, and revealed to thy servants as a light to lighten the Gentiles and the glory of thy people Israel. Therefore with Angels, &c.

73

Upon The Annunciation.

BECAUSE thou didst give Jesus Christ, thine only Son, to be born for us; who by the operation of the Holy Ghost was made very man, of the substance of the Blessed Virgin Mary his mother, and that without spot of sin, to make us clean from all sin. Therefore with Angels, &c.

From Ash Wednesday *until the* Saturday *before*
Passion Sunday *inclusive.*

BECAUSE thou hast given us the spirit of discipline, that we may triumph over the flesh, and live no longer unto ourselves but unto him who died for us and rose again. Therefore with Angels, &c.

From Passion Sunday *until the* Wednesday *before*
Easter *inclusive.*

BECAUSE thou didst give thine only Son, our Saviour Jesus Christ, to redeem mankind from the power of darkness; who, having finished the work thou gavest him to do, was lifted up upon the cross that he might draw all men unto himself, and, being made perfect through suffering, might become the author of eternal salvation to all of them that obey him. Therefore with Angels, &c.

Upon Maundy Thursday.

THROUGH Jesus Christ our Lord; who having loved his own which were in the world, loved them unto the end, and on the night before he suffered, sitting at meat with his disciples, did institute these holy mysteries; that we, receiving the benefits of his passion, and being quickened by his resurrection, might be made partakers of the divine nature. Therefore with Angels, &c.

Upon Easter Day, *and until the* Eve of
Ascension Day *inclusive.*

BUT chiefly are we bound to praise thee for the glorious resurrection of thy Son Jesus Christ our Lord: for he is the very Paschal Lamb which was offered for us, and hath taken away the sin of the world; who by his death hath destroyed death, and by his rising to life again hath restored to us everlasting life. Therefore with Angels, &c.

Upon Ascension Day, *and until the* Vigil of
Whitsunday *inclusive.*

THROUGH thy most dearly beloved Son Jesus Christ our Lord; who, after his most glorious resurrection, manifestly appeared to all his Apostles, and in their sight ascended up into heaven to prepare a place for us; that where he is, thither we might also ascend, and reign with him in glory. Therefore with Angels, &c.

Upon Pentecost *or* Whitsunday, *and six days after.*

THROUGH Jesus Christ our Lord; according to whose most true promise, the Holy Ghost came down *[as on this day] from heaven with a sudden great sound, as it had been a mighty wind, in the likeness of fiery tongues, lighting upon the Apostles, to teach them, and to lead them to *During the six days after Whitsunday say,* as at this time. all truth; giving them both the gift of tongues, and also boldness with fervent zeal constantly to preach the Gospel unto all nations; whereby we have been brought out of darkness and error into the clear light and true knowledge of thee, and of thy Son Jesus Christ. Therefore with Angels, &c.

Or this,

THROUGH Jesus Christ our Lord; who after that he had ascended up far above all the heavens, and was set down at the right hand of thy Majesty, did as at this time pour forth upon the universal Church thy holy and life-giving Spirit: that through his glorious power the joy of the everlasting Gospel might go forth into all the world; whereby we have been brought out of darkness and error into the clear light and true knowledge of thee, and of thy Son our Saviour Jesus Christ. Therefore with Angels, &c.

Upon the Feast of Trinity only.

WHO with thine only-begotten Son and the Holy Ghost art one God, one Lord, in Trinity of Persons and in Unity of Substance; for that which we believe of thy glory, O Father, the same we believe of the Son, and of the Holy Ghost, without any difference or inequality. Therefore with Angels, &c.

Upon the Feast of the Transfiguration.

BECAUSE thou hast made known to us the honour and glory of thy beloved Son, to whom before his passion thy voice bare witness on the holy Mount. Therefore with Angels, &c.

Upon Feasts of Apostles and Evangelists.

THROUGH Jesus Christ our Lord, who did vouchsafe to choose thy servant Saint *N.* [or thy servants Saint *N.* and Saint *N.*] to be of the company of the Apostles [*or* to be an Evangelist], by whose ministry thine elect might be gathered in from every nation, and thy Church instructed in the way that leadeth unto everlasting life. Therefore with Angels, &c.

Upon All Saints' Day, St. John Baptist's, St. Columba's, St. Kentigern's, St. Patrick's, St. Ninian's, and St. Margaret of Scotland's Days.

WHO in the multitude of thy Saints hast compassed us about with so great a cloud of witnesses, to the end that we, rejoicing in their fellowship, may run with patience the race that is set before us, and together with them receive the crown of glory that fadeth not away. Therefore with Angels, &c.

At the Consecration of Bishops, and Ordination of Priests and Deacons, and on Ember Days.

THROUGH Jesus Christ our Lord, the great Shepherd of the sheep; who, for the feeding and guidance of his flock, did appoint divers orders of ministers in his Church. Therefore with Angels, &c.

At the Dedication of a Church, *and* Anniversary of the
Dedication.

WHO in temples made with hands buildest up for thyself a spiritual temple made without hands. Therefore
with Angels, &c.

*The Proper Prefaces other than those for the Great Festivals are for permissive
use only.*

POST-COMMUNIONS

*for certain Festivals and Seasons, which may be said immediately
before the Blessing.*

Advent.

GRANT, O Almighty God, that as thy blessed Son
Jesus Christ at his first advent came to seek and to
save that which was lost, so at his second and glorious appearing he may find in us the fruits of the redemption which
he wrought; who liveth and reigneth, with thee and the
Holy Spirit, one God, world without end. *Amen.*

Christmas Day, *and until the* Eve of the
Epiphany *inclusive.*

O GOD, who hast given us grace at this time to celebrate
the birth of our Saviour Jesus Christ: We laud and
magnify thy glorious Name for the countless blessings which
he hath brought unto us; and we beseech thee to grant that
we may ever set forth thy praise in joyful obedience to thy
will; through the same Jesus Christ our Lord. *Amen.*

The Epiphany, *and seven days after.*

ALMIGHTY God, who at the baptism of thy blessed Son
Jesus Christ in the river Jordan didst manifest his
glorious Godhead: Grant, we beseech thee, that the brightness of his presence may shine in our hearts, and his glory
be set forth in our lives; through the same Jesus Christ
our Lord. *Amen.*

From Ash Wednesday *until the* Saturday *before* Passion Sunday *inclusive*.

O GOD, whose nature and property is ever to have mercy and to forgive: Receive our humble petitions; and though we be tied and bound with the chain of our sins, yet let the pitifulness of thy great mercy loose us; for the honour of Jesus Christ, our Mediator and Advocate. *Amen*.

From Passion Sunday *until* Maundy Thursday *inclusive*.

O GOD, who by the cross and passion of thy Son Jesus Christ didst save and deliver mankind: Grant that by stedfast faith in the merits of that holy sacrifice we may find help and salvation, and may triumph in the power of his victory; through the same Jesus Christ our Lord. *Amen*.

Easter Day, *and until the* Eve of Ascension Day *inclusive*.

O LORD God Almighty, whose blessed Son our Saviour Jesus Christ did on the third day rise triumphant over death: Raise us, we beseech thee, from the death of sin unto the life of righteousness, that we may seek those things which are above, where he sitteth on thy right hand in glory; and this we beg for the sake of the same thy Son Jesus Christ our Lord. *Amen*.

Ascension Day, *and until the* Vigil of Whitsunday *inclusive*.

A LMIGHTY God, whose blessed Son our Saviour Jesus Christ ascended far above all heavens that he might fill all things: Mercifully give us faith to perceive that according to his promise he abideth with his Church on earth, even unto the end of the world; through the same Jesus Christ our Lord. *Amen*.

Whitsunday, *and six days after*.

O ALMIGHTY God, who on the day of Pentecost didst send the Holy Ghost the Comforter to abide in thy Church unto the end: Bestow upon us and upon all thy faithful people his manifold gifts of grace, that with minds enlightened by his truth, and hearts purified by his presence, we may day by day be strengthened with power in the inward man; through Jesus Christ our Lord, who with thee and the same Spirit liveth and reigneth, one God, world without end. *Amen.*

Trinity Sunday.

O LORD God Almighty, Eternal, Immortal, Invisible, the mysteries of whose being are unsearchable: Accept, we beseech thee, our praises for the revelation which thou hast made of thyself, Father, Son, and Holy Ghost, three Persons, and one God; and mercifully grant, that ever holding fast this faith, we may magnify thy glorious Name; who livest and reignest, one God, world without end. *Amen.*

Saints' Days, *except* All Saints' Day.

O ALMIGHTY God, who hast knit together thine elect in one communion and fellowship, in the mystical body of thy Son Christ our Lord: Grant us grace so to follow thy blessed Saints in all virtuous and godly living, that we may come to those unspeakable joys, which thou hast prepared for them that unfeignedly love thee; through Jesus Christ our Lord. *Amen.*

GENERAL POST-COMMUNIONS

O LORD our God, thou Saviour of the world, through whom we have celebrated these Holy Mysteries: Receive our humble thanksgiving, and of thy great mercy vouchsafe to sanctify us evermore in body and soul; who livest and reignest with the Father and the Holy Spirit, one God, world without end. *Amen.*

A LMIGHTY God, who hast promised to hear the petitions of them that ask in thy Son's Name: We beseech thee mercifully to incline thine ears to us that have made now our prayers and supplications unto thee; and grant that those things which we have faithfully asked according to thy will may effectually be obtained, to the relief of our necessity and to the setting forth of thy glory; through Jesus Christ our Lord. *Amen.*

COLLECTS

which may be said after the Collect of the Day, or before the Blessing.

O ALMIGHTY Lord, and Everlasting God, vouchsafe, we beseech thee, to direct, sanctify, and govern both our hearts and bodies, in the ways of thy laws, and in the works of thy commandments; that through thy most mighty protection, both here and ever, we may be preserved in body and soul; through our Lord and Saviour Jesus Christ. *Amen.*

O ALMIGHTY Father, well-spring of life to all things that have being, from amid the unwearied praises of Cherubin and Seraphin who stand about thy throne of light which no man can approach unto: Give ear, we humbly beseech thee, to the supplications of thy people who put their sure trust in thy mercy; through Jesus Christ our Lord. *Amen.*

O LORD Jesus Christ, before whose judgement-seat we must all appear and give account of the things done in the body: Grant, we beseech thee, that when the books are opened in that day, the faces of thy servants may not be ashamed; through thy merits, O blessed Saviour, who livest and reignest with the Father and the Holy Spirit, one God, world without end. *Amen.*

A SSIST us mercifully, O Lord, in these our supplications and prayers, and dispose the way of thy servants towards the attainment of everlasting salvation; that among all the changes and chances of this mortal life, they may ever be defended by thy most gracious and ready help; through Jesus Christ our Lord. *Amen.*

P REVENT us, O Lord, in all our doings with thy most gracious favour, and further us with thy continual help; that in all our works begun, continued, and ended in thee, we may glorify thy holy Name, and finally by thy mercy obtain everlasting life; through Jesus Christ our Lord. *Amen.*

ALMIGHTY God, the fountain of all wisdom, who knowest our necessities before we ask, and our ignorance in asking: We beseech thee to have compassion upon our infirmities; and those things, which for our unworthiness we dare not, and for our blindness we cannot ask, vouchsafe to give us, for the worthiness of thy Son Jesus Christ our Lord. *Amen.*

REMEMBER, O Lord, what thou hast wrought in us, and not what we deserve; and as thou hast called us to thy service, make us worthy of our calling; through Jesus Christ our Lord. *Amen.*

O GOD the King of Saints, we praise and magnify thy holy Name for all thy servants who have finished their course in thy faith and fear, for the Blessed Virgin Mary, for the holy Patriarchs, Prophets, Apostles, and Martyrs, and for all other thy righteous servants; and we beseech thee that, encouraged by their example, strengthened by their fellowship, and aided by their prayers, we may attain unto everlasting life; through the merits of thy Son Jesus Christ our Lord. *Amen.*

O ETERNAL Lord God, who holdest all souls in life: We beseech thee to shed forth upon all the faithful departed the bright beams of thy light and heavenly comfort; and grant that they, and we with them, may at length attain to the joys of thine eternal kingdom; through Jesus Christ our Lord. *Amen.*

EXHORTATIONS BEFORE THE HOLY COMMUNION

DEARLY beloved, on —— I purpose, through God's assistance, to administer to all such as shall be religiously and devoutly disposed the most comfortable Sacrament of the Body and Blood of Christ; to be by them received in remembrance of his meritorious cross and passion; whereby alone we obtain remission of our sins, and are made partakers of the kingdom of heaven. Wherefore it is our duty to render most humble and hearty thanks to Almighty God our heavenly Father, for that he hath given his Son our Saviour Jesus Christ, not only to die for us, but also to be our spiritual food and sustenance in that holy Sacrament. Which being so divine and comfortable a thing to them who receive it worthily, and so dangerous to them that will presume to receive it unworthily; my duty is to exhort you in the mean season to consider the dignity of that holy Mystery, and the great peril of the unworthy receiving thereof; and so to search and examine your own consciences, (and that not lightly, and after the manner of dissemblers with God; but so) that ye may come holy and clean to such a heavenly Feast, in the marriage-garment required by God in Holy Scripture, and be received as worthy partakers of that Holy Table.

The way and means thereto is: First, to examine your life and conduct by the rule of God's commandments; and whereinsoever ye shall perceive yourselves to have offended, either by will, word, or deed, there to bewail your own sinfulness, and to confess yourselves to Almighty God, with full purpose of amendment of life. And if ye shall perceive your offences to be such as are not only against God, but also against your neighbours; Then ye shall reconcile yourselves unto them; being ready to make restitution and satisfaction, according to the uttermost of your powers, for all injuries and wrongs done by you to any other; and being likewise ready to forgive others that have offended you, as you would have forgiveness of your offences at God's hand. Therefore if any of you be a blasphemer of God, an hinderer or slanderer of his word, an adulterer, or be in malice, or envy, or in any other grievous crime, repent you of your sins, or else come not to that Holy Table.

And because it is requisite, that no man should come to the Holy Communion, but with a full trust in God's mercy, and with a quiet conscience; therefore if there be any of you, who by this means cannot quiet his own conscience herein, but requireth further comfort or counsel, let him come to me, or to some other discreet and learned Minister of God's word, and open his grief; that by the ministry of God's holy word he may receive the benefit of absolution, together with spiritual counsel and advice, to the quieting of his conscience, and avoiding of all scruple and doubtfulness.

Note. Such as shall be satisfied with a general Confession should not be offended with them that do use, to their further satisfying, confession to the Priest; and those also which think needful or convenient, for the quietness of their own consciences, particularly to open their sins to the Priest, should not be offended with them that are satisfied with their humble confession to God, and the general Confession to the Church. But in all things everyone should follow and keep the rule of charity, and be satisfied with his own conscience, not judging other men's minds and consciences, whereas he hath no warrant of God's word to the same.

The following may be said, instead of the former, in case the Priest shall see the people negligent to come to the Holy Communion.

DEARLY beloved brethren, on —— I intend, by God's grace, to celebrate the Lord's Supper: unto which, in God's behalf, I bid you all that are here present; and beseech you, for the Lord Jesus Christ's sake, that ye will not refuse to come thereto, being so lovingly called and bidden by God himself. Ye know how grievous and unkind a thing it is, when a man hath prepared a rich feast, decked his table with all kind of provision, so that there lacketh nothing but the guests to sit down; and yet they who are called (without any cause) most unthankfully refuse to come. Which of you in such a case would not be moved? Who would not think a great injury and wrong done unto him? Wherefore, most dearly beloved in Christ, take ye good heed, lest ye, withdrawing yourselves from this holy Supper, provoke God's indignation against you. It is an easy matter for a man to say, I will not communicate, because I am otherwise hindered with worldly business. But such excuses are not so easily accepted and allowed before God. If any man say, I am a grievous sinner, and therefore am afraid to come: wherefore then do ye not repent and amend? When God calleth you, are ye not ashamed to say ye will not come? When ye should return to God, will ye excuse yourselves, and say ye are not ready? Consider earnestly with yourselves how little such feigned excuses will avail before God. They that refused the feast in the Gospel, because they had bought a farm, or would try their yokes of oxen, or because they were married, were not so excused, but counted unworthy of the heavenly Feast. I, for my part, shall be ready; and according to mine Office, I bid you in the Name of God, I call you in Christ's behalf, I exhort you, as ye love your own salvation, that ye will be partakers of this Holy Communion. And as the Son of God did vouchsafe to yield up his soul by death upon the cross for your salvation; so it is your duty to receive the Communion in remembrance of the sacrifice of his death, as he himself hath commanded: which if ye shall neglect to do, consider with yourselves how great injury ye do unto God, and how sore punishment hangeth over your heads for the same; when ye wilfully abstain from the Lord's Table, and separate from your brethren, who come to feed on the banquet of that most heavenly food. These things if ye earnestly consider, ye will by God's grace return to a better mind: for the obtaining whereof we shall not cease to make our humble petitions unto Almighty God our heavenly Father.

EXHORTATION AT THE HOLY COMMUNION

DEARLY beloved in the Lord, ye that mind to come to the Holy Communion of the Body and Blood of our Saviour Christ, must consider what Saint Paul writeth to the Corinthians; how he exhorteth all persons diligently to try and examine themselves, before they presume to eat of that Bread, and drink of that Cup. For as the benefit is great, if with a true penitent heart and living faith we receive that holy Sacrament; (for then we spiritually eat the Flesh of Christ, and drink his Blood; then we dwell in Christ, and Christ in us; we are one with Christ, and Christ with us;) so is the danger great, if we receive the same unworthily. For then we are guilty of the Body and Blood of Christ our Saviour; we eat and drink judgement to ourselves, not discerning the Lord's Body; we kindle God's wrath against us; we provoke him to plague us with divers diseases, and sundry kinds of death. Judge therefore yourselves, brethren, that ye be not judged of the Lord; repent you truly for your sins past; have a living and stedfast faith in Christ our Saviour; amend your lives, and be in perfect charity with all men: so shall ye be meet partakers of those holy Mysteries. And, above all things, ye must give most humble and hearty thanks to God, the Father, the Son, and the Holy Ghost, for the redemption of the world by the death and passion of our Saviour Christ, both God and man; who did humble himself even to the death upon the cross for us miserable sinners, who lay in darkness and the shadow of death, that he might make us the children of God, and exalt us to everlasting life. And to the end that we should always remember the exceeding great love of our Master and only Saviour Jesus Christ thus dying for us, and the innumerable benefits which by his precious Blood-shedding he hath obtained to us, he hath instituted and ordained holy Mysteries, as pledges of his love, and for a continual remembrance of his death, to our great and endless comfort. To him therefore, with the Father and the Holy Ghost, let us give (as we are most bounden) continual thanks, submitting ourselves wholly to his holy will and pleasure, and studying to serve him in true holiness and righteousness all the days of our life. *Amen.*

This Exhortation may also be used at other times.

NOTE

In certain churches in Scotland where it has long been in use, the 1764 text of the Scottish Liturgy is still permitted. In structure this corresponds with the present liturgy of 1929, but the Invocation in the Canon is as follows:

> And we most humbly beseech thee, O merciful Father, to hear us, and of thy almighty goodness vouchsafe to bless and sanctify with thy word and Holy Spirit, these thy gifts and creatures of bread and wine, that they may become the body and blood of thy most dearly beloved Son.

In the Oblation which precedes it, the words 'and looking for his coming again with power and great glory' are not present.

As the 1764 liturgy, like all the 'wee bookies' of which it was one, was not a complete service, but a non-juring revision of the office from the Offertory onwards, there was no authorized text of the earlier portion of the Scottish liturgy until 1912. In actual practice[1] the corresponding part of the English 1662 was almost invariably used save that the Summary of the Law was frequently substituted for the Decalogue, and the collect 'O Almighty Lord, and everlasting God . . .' (the second of the final collects in 1662) was often said instead of the collect for the King; this is reflected in the American Rite, p. 91.

[1] Much valuable information will be found in *Traditional Customs connected with the Scottish Liturgy*, by F. C. Eeles (Oxford University Press, for the Alcuin Club).

THE AMERICAN RITE
(1935)

THE ORDER FOR THE
ADMINISTRATION OF THE LORD'S SUPPER

OR

HOLY COMMUNION

¶ At the Communion-time the Holy Table shall have upon it a fair white linen cloth. And the Priest, standing reverently before the Holy Table, shall say the Lord's Prayer and the Collect following, the People kneeling; but the Lord's Prayer may be omitted at the discretion of the Priest.

OUR Father, who art in heaven, Hallowed be thy Name. Thy kingdom come. Thy will be done, On earth as it is in heaven. Give us this day our daily bread. And forgive us our trespasses, As we forgive those who trespass against us. And lead us not into temptation, But deliver us from evil. Amen.

The Collect.

ALMIGHTY God, unto whom all hearts are open, all desires known, and from whom no secrets are hid; Cleanse the thoughts of our hearts by the inspiration of thy Holy Spirit, that we may perfectly love thee, and worthily magnify thy holy Name; through Christ our Lord. *Amen.*

¶ Then shall the Priest, turning to the People, rehearse distinctly The Ten Commandments; and the People, still kneeling, shall, after every Commandment, ask God mercy for their transgressions for the time past, and grace to keep the law for the time to come.

¶ And NOTE, *That in rehearsing The Ten Commandments, the Priest may omit that part of the Commandment which is inset.*

¶ The Decalogue may be omitted, provided it be said at least one Sunday in each month. But NOTE, *That whenever it is omitted, the Priest shall say the Summary of the Law, beginning,* Hear what our Lord Jesus Christ saith.

The Decalogue.

GOD spake these words, and said:
I am the LORD thy God; Thou shalt have none other gods but me.

Lord, have mercy upon us, and incline our hearts to keep this law.

Thou shalt not make to thyself any graven image, nor the likeness of any thing that is in heaven above, or in the earth beneath, or in the water under the earth; thou shalt not bow down to them, nor worship them;

for I the LORD thy God am a jealous God, and visit the sins of the fathers upon the children, unto the third and fourth generation of them that hate me; and show mercy unto thousands in them that love me and keep my commandments.

Lord, have mercy upon us, and incline our hearts to keep this law.

Thou shalt not take the Name of the LORD thy God in vain;

for the LORD will not hold him guiltless, that taketh his Name in vain.

Lord, have mercy upon us, and incline our hearts to keep this law.

Remember that thou keep holy the Sabbath-day.

Six days shalt thou labour, and do all that thou hast to do; but the seventh day is the Sabbath of the LORD thy God. In it thou shalt do no manner of work; thou, and thy son, and thy daughter, thy man-servant, and thy maid-servant, thy cattle, and the stranger that is within thy gates. For in six days the LORD made heaven and earth, the sea, and all that in them is, and rested the seventh day: wherefore the LORD blessed the seventh day, and hallowed it.

Lord, have mercy upon us, and incline our hearts to keep this law.

Honour thy father and thy mother;

that thy days may be long in the land which the LORD thy God giveth thee.

Lord, have mercy upon us, and incline our hearts to keep this law.

Thou shalt do no murder.

Lord, have mercy upon us, and incline our hearts to keep this law.

Thou shalt not commit adultery.

Lord, have mercy upon us, and incline our hearts to keep this law.

Thou shalt not steal.

Lord, have mercy upon us, and incline our hearts to keep this law.

Thou shalt not bear false witness against thy neighbour.

Lord, have mercy upon us, and incline our hearts to keep this law.

Thou shalt not covet

thy neighbour's house, thou shalt not covet thy neighbour's wife, nor his servant, nor his maid, nor his ox, nor his ass, nor any thing that is his.

Lord, have mercy upon us, and write all these thy laws in our hearts, we beseech thee.

¶ *Then may the Priest say,*

Hear what our Lord Jesus Christ saith.

THOU shalt love the Lord thy God with all thy heart, and with all thy soul, and with all thy mind. This is the first and great commandment. And the second is like unto it; Thou shalt love thy neighbour as thyself. On these two commandments hang all the Law and the Prophets.

¶ *Here, if the Decalogue hath been omitted, shall be said,*

Lord, have mercy upon us.
Christ, have mercy upon us.
Lord, have mercy upon us.

¶ *Then the Priest may say,*

O ALMIGHTY Lord, and everlasting God, vouchsafe, we beseech thee, to direct, sanctify, and govern, both our hearts and bodies, in the ways of thy laws, and in the works of thy commandments; that, through thy most mighty protection, both here and ever, we may be preserved in body and soul; through our Lord and Saviour Jesus Christ. *Amen.*

¶ *Here shall be said,*

The Lord be with you.
Answer. And with thy spirit.
Minister. Let us pray.

¶ *Then shall the Priest say the Collect of the Day. And after the Collect the Minister appointed shall read the Epistle, first saying,* The Epistle is written in the —— Chapter of ——, beginning at the —— Verse. *The Epistle ended, he shall say,* Here endeth the Epistle.

¶ *Here may be sung a Hymn or an Anthem.*

¶ *Then, all the People standing, the Minister appointed shall read the Gospel, first saying,* The Holy Gospel is written in the —— Chapter of ——, beginning at the —— Verse.

¶ Here shall be said,

Glory be to thee, O Lord.

¶ And after the Gospel may be said,

Praise be to thee, O Christ.

¶ Then shall be said the Creed commonly called the Nicene, or else the Apostles' Creed; but the Creed may be omitted, if it hath been said immediately before in Morning Prayer; Provided, That the Nicene Creed shall be said on Christmas Day, Easter Day, Ascension Day, Whitsunday, and Trinity Sunday.

I BELIEVE in one God the Father Almighty, Maker of heaven and earth, And of all things visible and invisible: And in one Lord Jesus Christ, the only-begotten Son of God; Begotten of his Father before all worlds, God of God, Light of Light, Very God of very God; Begotten, not made; Being of one substance with the Father; By whom all things were made: Who for us men and for our salvation came down from heaven, And was incarnate by the Holy Ghost of the Virgin Mary, And was made man: And was crucified also for us under Pontius Pilate; He suffered and was buried: And the third day he rose again according to the Scriptures: And ascended into heaven, And sitteth on the right hand of the Father: And he shall come again, with glory, to judge both the quick and the dead; Whose kingdom shall have no end.

And I believe in the Holy Ghost, The Lord, and Giver of Life, Who proceedeth from the Father and the Son; Who with the Father and the Son together is worshipped and glorified; Who spake by the Prophets: And I believe one Catholic and Apostolic Church: I acknowledge one Baptism for the remission of sins: And I look for the Resurrection of the dead: And the Life of the world to come. Amen.

¶ Then shall be declared unto the People what Holy Days, or Fasting Days, are in the week following to be observed; and (if occasion be) shall Notice be given of the Communion, and of the Banns of Matrimony, and of other matters to be published.

¶ Here, or immediately after the Creed, may be said the Bidding Prayer, or other authorized prayers and intercessions.

¶ *Then followeth the Sermon. After which, the Priest, when there is a Communion, shall return to the Holy Table, and begin the Offertory, saying one or more of these Sentences following, as he thinketh most convenient.*

REMEMBER the words of the Lord Jesus, how he said, It is more blessed to give than to receive. *Acts* xx. 35.

Let your light so shine before men, that they may see your good works, and glorify your Father which is in heaven. *St. Matt.* v. 16.

Lay not up for yourselves treasures upon earth, where moth and rust doth corrupt, and where thieves break through and steal: but lay up for yourselves treasures in heaven, where neither moth nor rust doth corrupt, and where thieves do not break through nor steal. *St. Matt.* vi. 19, 20.

Not every one that saith unto me, Lord, Lord, shall enter into the kingdom of heaven; but he that doeth the will of my Father which is in heaven. *St. Matt.* vii. 21.

He that soweth little shall reap little; and he that soweth plenteously shall reap plenteously. Let every man do according as he is disposed in his heart, not grudgingly, or of necessity; for God loveth a cheerful giver. *2 Cor.* ix. 6, 7.

While we have time, let us do good unto all men; and especially unto them that are of the household of faith. *Gal.* vi. 10.

God is not unrighteous, that he will forget your works, and labour that proceedeth of love; which love ye have showed for his Name's sake, who have ministered unto the saints, and yet do minister. *Heb.* vi. 10.

To do good, and to distribute, forget not; for with such sacrifices God is well pleased. *Heb.* xiii. 16.

Whoso hath this world's good, and seeth his brother have need, and shutteth up his compassion from him, how dwelleth the love of God in him? 1 *St. John* iii. 17.

Be merciful after thy power. If thou hast much, give plenteously; if thou hast little, do thy diligence gladly to give of that little: for so gatherest thou thyself a good reward in the day of necessity. *Tobit* iv. 8, 9.

And the King shall answer and say unto them, Verily I say unto you, Inasmuch as ye have done it unto one of the least of these my brethren, ye have done it unto me. *St. Matt.* xxv. 40.

How then shall they call on him in whom they have not believed? and how shall they believe in him of whom they have not heard? and how shall they hear without a preacher? and how shall they preach, except they be sent? *Rom.* x. 14, 15.

Jesus said unto them, The harvest truly is plenteous, but the labourers are few: pray ye therefore the Lord of the harvest, that he send forth labourers into his harvest. *St. Luke* x. 2.

Ye shall not appear before the LORD empty; every man shall give as he is able, according to the blessing of the LORD thy God which he hath given thee. *Deut.* xvi. 16, 17.

Thine, O LORD, is the greatness, and the power, and the glory, and the victory, and the majesty: for all that is in the heaven and in the earth is thine; thine is the kingdom, O LORD, and thou art exalted as head above all. *1 Chron.* xxix. 11.

All things come of thee, O LORD, and of thine own have we given thee. *1 Chron.* xxix. 14.

¶ *And* NOTE, *That these Sentences may be used on any other occasion of Public Worship when the Offerings of the People are to be received.*

¶ *The Deacons, Church-wardens, or other fit persons appointed for that purpose, shall receive the Alms for the Poor, and other Offerings of the People, in a decent Basin to be provided by the Parish; and reverently bring it to the Priest, who shall humbly present and place it upon the Holy Table.*

¶ *And the Priest shall then offer, and shall place upon the Holy Table, the Bread and the Wine.*

¶ *And when the Alms and Oblations are being received and presented, there may be sung a Hymn, or an Offertory Anthem in the words of Holy Scripture or of the Book of Common Prayer, under the direction of the Priest.*

¶ Here the Priest may ask the secret intercessions of the Congregation for any who have desired the prayers of the Church.

¶ Then shall the Priest say,

Let us pray for the whole state of Christ's Church.

ALMIGHTY and everliving God, who by thy holy Apostle hast taught us to make prayers, and supplications, and to give thanks for all men; We humbly beseech thee most mercifully to accept our [*alms and*] oblations, and to receive these our prayers, which we offer unto thy Divine Majesty; beseeching thee to inspire continually the Universal Church with the spirit of truth, unity, and concord: And grant that all those who do confess thy holy Name may agree in the truth of thy holy Word, and live in unity and godly love.

We beseech thee also, so to direct and dispose the hearts of all Christian Rulers, that they may truly and impartially administer justice, to the punishment of wickedness and vice, and to the maintenance of thy true religion, and virtue.

Give grace, O heavenly Father, to all Bishops and other Ministers, that they may, both by their life and doctrine, set forth thy true and lively Word, and rightly and duly administer thy holy Sacraments.

And to all thy People give thy heavenly grace; and especially to this congregation here present; that, with meek heart and due reverence, they may hear, and receive thy holy Word; truly serving thee in holiness and righteousness all the days of their life.

And we most humbly beseech thee, of thy goodness, O Lord, to comfort and succour all those who, in this transitory life, are in trouble, sorrow, need, sickness, or any other adversity.

And we also bless thy holy Name for all thy servants departed this life in thy faith and fear; beseeching thee to grant them continual growth in thy love and service, and to give us grace so to follow their good examples, that with

95

them we may be partakers of thy heavenly kingdom. Grant this, O Father, for Jesus Christ's sake, our only Mediator and Advocate. *Amen.*

¶ *Then shall the Priest say to those who come to receive the Holy Communion,*

YE who do truly and earnestly repent you of your sins, and are in love and charity with your neighbours, and intend to lead a new life, following the commandments of God, and walking from henceforth in his holy ways; Draw near with faith, and take this holy Sacrament to your comfort; and make your humble confession to Almighty God, devoutly kneeling.

¶ *Then shall this General Confession be made, by the Priest and all those who are minded to receive the Holy Communion, humbly kneeling.*

ALMIGHTY God, Father of our Lord Jesus Christ, Maker of all things, Judge of all men; We acknowledge and bewail our manifold sins and wickedness, Which we, from time to time, most grievously have committed, By thought, word, and deed, Against thy Divine Majesty, Provoking most justly thy wrath and indignation against us. We do earnestly repent, And are heartily sorry for these our misdoings; The remembrance of them is grievous unto us; The burden of them is intolerable. Have mercy upon us, Have mercy upon us, most merciful Father; For thy Son our Lord Jesus Christ's sake, Forgive us all that is past; And grant that we may ever hereafter Serve and please thee In newness of life, To the honour and glory of thy Name; Through Jesus Christ our Lord. Amen.

¶ *Then shall the Priest (the Bishop if he be present) stand up, and turning to the People, say,*

ALMIGHTY God, our heavenly Father, who of his great mercy hath promised forgiveness of sins to all those who with hearty repentance and true faith turn unto him; Have mercy upon you; pardon and deliver you from all your sins; confirm and strengthen you in all goodness; and bring you to everlasting life; through Jesus Christ our Lord. *Amen.*

¶ *Then shall the Priest say,*

Hear what comfortable words our Saviour Christ saith unto all who truly turn to him.

COME unto me, all ye that travail and are heavy laden, and I will refresh you. *St. Matt.* xi. 28.

So God loved the world, that he gave his only-begotten Son, to the end that all that believe in him should not perish, but have everlasting life. *St. John* iii. 16.

Hear also what Saint Paul saith.

This is a true saying, and worthy of all men to be received, That Christ Jesus came into the world to save sinners.

1 *Tim.* i. 15.

Hear also what Saint John saith.

If any man sin, we have an Advocate with the Father, Jesus Christ the righteous; and he is the Propitiation for our sins. 1 *St. John* ii. 1, 2.

¶ *After which the Priest shall proceed, saying,*

Lift up your hearts.

Answer. We lift them up unto the Lord.

Priest. Let us give thanks unto our Lord God.

Answer. It is meet and right so to do.

¶ *Then shall the Priest turn to the Holy Table, and say,*

IT is very meet, right, and our bounden duty, that we should at all times, and in all places, give thanks unto thee, O Lord, Holy Father, Almighty, Everlasting God.

¶ *Here shall follow the Proper Preface, according to the time, if there be any specially appointed; or else immediately shall be said or sung by the Priest,*

THEREFORE with Angels and Archangels, and with all the company of heaven, we laud and magnify thy glorious Name; evermore praising thee, and saying,

HOLY, HOLY, HOLY, Lord God of hosts, Heaven and earth are full of thy ¶ *Priest and People.* glory: Glory be to thee, O Lord Most High. Amen.

H

PROPER PREFACES

CHRISTMAS.

¶ Upon Christmas Day, and seven days after.

BECAUSE thou didst give Jesus Christ, thine only Son, to be born as at this time for us; who, by the operation of the Holy Ghost, was made very man, of the substance of the Virgin Mary his mother; and that without spot of sin, to make us clean from all sin.

Therefore with Angels, &c.

EPIPHANY.

¶ Upon the Epiphany, and seven days after.

THROUGH Jesus Christ our Lord; who, in substance of our mortal flesh, manifested forth his glory; that he might bring us out of darkness into his own glorious light.

Therefore with Angels, &c.

PURIFICATION, ANNUNCIATION, AND TRANSFIGURATION.

¶ Upon the Feasts of the Purification, Annunciation, and Transfiguration.

BECAUSE in the Mystery of the Word made flesh, thou hast caused a new light to shine in our hearts, to give the knowledge of thy glory in the face of thy Son Jesus Christ our Lord.

Therefore with Angels, &c.

EASTER.

¶ Upon Easter Day, and seven days after.

BUT chiefly are we bound to praise thee for the glorious Resurrection of thy Son Jesus Christ our Lord: for he is the very Paschal Lamb, which was offered for us, and hath taken away the sin of the world; who by his death hath destroyed death, and by his rising to life again hath restored to us everlasting life.

Therefore with Angels, &c.

Ascension.

¶ Upon Ascension Day, and seven days after.

THROUGH thy most dearly beloved Son Jesus Christ our Lord; who, after his most glorious Resurrection, manifestly appeared to all his Apostles, and in their sight ascended up into heaven, to prepare a place for us; that where he is, thither we might also ascend, and reign with him in glory.

Therefore with Angels, &c.

Whitsuntide.

¶ Upon Whitsunday, and six days after.

THROUGH Jesus Christ our Lord; according to whose most true promise, the Holy Ghost came down as at this time from heaven, lighting upon the disciples, to teach them, and to lead them into all truth; giving them boldness with fervent zeal constantly to preach the Gospel unto all nations; whereby we have been brought out of darkness and error into the clear light and true knowledge of thee, and of thy Son Jesus Christ.

Therefore with Angels, &c.

Trinity Sunday.

¶ Upon the Feast of Trinity only.

WHO, with thine only-begotten Son, and the Holy Ghost, art one God, one Lord, in Trinity of Persons and in Unity of Substance. For that which we believe of thy glory, O Father, the same we believe of the Son, and of the Holy Ghost, without any difference of inequality.

Therefore with Angels, &c.

¶ Or this.

FOR the precious death and merits of thy Son Jesus Christ our Lord, and for the sending to us of the Holy Ghost, the Comforter; who are one with thee in thy Eternal Godhead.

Therefore with Angels, &c.

ALL SAINTS.

¶ Upon All Saints' Day, and seven days after.

WHO, in the multitude of thy Saints, hast compassed us about with so great a cloud of witnesses that we, rejoicing in their fellowship, may run with patience the race that is set before us, and, together with them, may receive the crown of glory that fadeth not away.

Therefore with Angels and Archangels, and with all the company of heaven, we laud and magnify thy glorious Name; evermore praising thee, and saying,

HOLY, HOLY, HOLY, Lord God of hosts, Heaven and earth are full of thy glory: Glory be to thee, O Lord Most High. Amen. *¶ Priest and People,*

¶ When the Priest, standing before the Holy Table, hath so ordered the Bread and Wine, that he may with the more readiness and decency break the Bread before the People, and take the Cup into his hands, he shall say the Prayer of Consecration, as followeth.

ALL glory be to thee, Almighty God, our heavenly Father, for that thou, of thy tender mercy, didst give thine only Son Jesus Christ to suffer death upon the Cross for our redemption; who made there (by his one oblation of himself once offered) a full, perfect, and sufficient sacrifice, oblation, and satisfaction, for the sins of the whole world; and did institute, and in his holy Gospel command us to continue, a perpetual memory of that his precious death and sacrifice, until his coming again: For in the night in which he was betrayed, (*a*) he took Bread; and when he had given thanks, (*b*) he brake it, and gave it to his disciples, saying, Take, eat, (*c*) this is my Body, which is given for you; Do this in remembrance of me. Likewise, after supper, (*d*) he took the Cup; and when he had given thanks, he gave it to them, saying, Drink ye all of this; for (*e*) this is my Blood of the New Testament,

(*a*) *Here the Priest is to take the Paten into his hands.*

(*b*) *And here to break the Bread.*

(*c*) *And here to lay his hand upon all the Bread.*

(*d*) *Here he is to take the Cup into his hands.*

(*e*) *And here he is to lay his hand upon every vessel in which there is any Wine to be consecrated.*

which is shed for you, and for many, for the remission of sins; Do this, as oft as ye shall drink it, in remembrance of me.

WHEREFORE, O Lord and heavenly Father, according to the institution of thy *The Oblation.* dearly beloved Son our Saviour Jesus Christ, we, thy humble servants, do celebrate and make here before thy Divine Majesty, with these thy holy gifts, which we now offer unto thee, the memorial thy Son hath commanded us to make; having in remembrance his blessed passion and precious death, his mighty resurrection and glorious ascension; rendering unto thee most hearty thanks for the innumerable benefits procured unto us by the same.

AND we most humbly beseech thee, O merciful Father, to hear us; and, of thy *The Invocation.* almighty goodness, vouchsafe to bless and sanctify, with thy Word and Holy Spirit, these thy gifts and creatures of bread and wine; that we, receiving them according to thy Son our Saviour Jesus Christ's holy institution, in remembrance of his death and passion, may be partakers of his most blessed Body and Blood.

AND we earnestly desire thy fatherly goodness, mercifully to accept this our sacrifice of praise and thanksgiving; most humbly beseeching thee to grant that, by the merits and death of thy Son Jesus Christ, and through faith in his blood, we, and all thy whole Church, may obtain remission of our sins, and all other benefits of his passion. And here we offer and present unto thee, O Lord, our selves, our souls and bodies, to be a reasonable, holy, and living sacrifice unto thee; humbly beseeching thee, that we, and all others who shall be partakers of this Holy Communion, may worthily receive the most precious Body and Blood of thy Son Jesus Christ, be filled with thy grace and heavenly benediction, and made one body with him, that he may dwell in us, and we in him. And although we are unworthy, through our manifold sins, to offer unto thee any sacrifice; yet we beseech thee to accept this our bounden duty and service; not weighing our merits, but pardoning our offences, through Jesus Christ our Lord; by whom, and with whom, in the unity of the Holy Ghost, all honour and glory be unto thee, O Father Almighty, world without end. *Amen.*

And now, as our Saviour Christ hath taught us, we are bold to say,

OUR Father, who art in heaven, Hallowed be thy Name. Thy kingdom come. Thy will be done, On earth as it is in heaven. Give us this day our daily bread. And forgive us our trespasses, As we forgive those who trespass against us. And lead us not into temptation, But deliver us from evil. For thine is the kingdom, and the power, and the glory, for ever and ever. Amen.

¶ *Then shall the Priest, kneeling down at the Lord's Table, say, in the name of all those who shall receive the Communion, this Prayer following.*

WE do not presume to come to this thy Table, O merciful Lord, trusting in our own righteousness, but in thy manifold and great mercies. We are not worthy so much as to gather up the crumbs under thy Table. But thou art the same Lord, whose property is always to have mercy: Grant us therefore, gracious Lord, so to eat the flesh of thy dear Son Jesus Christ, and to drink his blood, that our sinful bodies may be made clean by his body, and our souls washed through his most precious blood, and that we may evermore dwell in him, and he in us. *Amen.*

¶ *Here may be sung a Hymn.*

¶ *Then shall the Priest first receive the Holy Communion in both kinds himself, and proceed to deliver the same to the Bishops, Priests, and Deacons, in like manner, (if any be present,) and, after that, to the People also in order, into their hands, all devoutly kneeling. And sufficient opportunity shall be given to those present to communicate. And when he delivereth the Bread, he shall say,*

THE Body of our Lord Jesus Christ, which was given for thee, preserve thy body and soul unto everlasting life. Take and eat this in remembrance that Christ died for thee, and feed on him in thy heart by faith, with thanksgiving.

¶ *And the Minister who delivereth the Cup shall say,*

THE Blood of our Lord Jesus Christ, which was shed for thee, preserve thy body and soul unto everlasting life. Drink this in remembrance that Christ's Blood was shed for thee, and be thankful.

¶ *If the consecrated Bread or Wine be spent before all have communicated, the Priest is to consecrate more, according to the Form before prescribed; beginning at,* All glory be to thee, Almighty God, *and ending with these words,* partakers of his most blessed Body and Blood.

¶ *When all have communicated, the Priest shall return to the Lord's Table, and reverently place upon it what remaineth of the consecrated Elements, covering the same with a fair linen cloth.*

¶ *Then shall the Priest say,*

Let us pray.

ALMIGHTY and everliving God, we most heartily thank thee, for that thou dost vouchsafe to feed us who have duly received these holy mysteries, with the spiritual food of the most precious Body and Blood of thy Son our Saviour Jesus Christ; and dost assure us thereby of thy favour and goodness towards us; and that we are very members incorporate in the mystical body of thy Son, which is the blessed company of all faithful people; and are also heirs through hope of thy everlasting kingdom, by the merits of his most precious death and passion. And we humbly beseech thee, O heavenly Father, so to assist us with thy grace, that we may continue in that holy fellowship, and do all such good works as thou hast prepared for us to walk in; through Jesus Christ our Lord, to whom, with thee and the Holy Ghost, be all honour and glory, world without end. *Amen.*

¶ *Then shall be said the Gloria in excelsis, all standing, or some proper Hymn.*

GLORY be to God on high, and on earth peace, good will towards men. We praise thee, we bless thee, we worship thee, we glorify thee, we give thanks to thee for thy great glory, O Lord God, heavenly King, God the Father Almighty.

O Lord, the only-begotten Son, Jesus Christ; O Lord God, Lamb of God, Son of the Father, that takest away the sins of the world, have mercy upon us. Thou that takest away the sins of the world, receive our prayer. Thou that sittest at the right hand of God the Father, have mercy upon us.

For thou only art holy; thou only art the Lord; thou only, O Christ, with the Holy Ghost, art most high in the glory of God the Father. Amen.

¶ *Then, the People kneeling, the Priest (the Bishop if he be present) shall let them depart with this Blessing.*

THE Peace of God, which passeth all understanding, keep your hearts and minds in the knowledge and love of God, and of his Son Jesus Christ our Lord: And the Blessing of God Almighty, the Father, the Son, and the Holy Ghost, be amongst you, and remain with you always. *Amen.*

GENERAL RUBRICS

¶ *In the absence of a Priest, a Deacon may say all that is before appointed unto the end of the Gospel.*

¶ *Upon the Sundays and other Holy Days, (though there be no Sermon or Communion,) may be said all that is appointed at the Communion, unto the end of the Gospel, concluding with the Blessing.*

¶ *And if any of the consecrated Bread and Wine remain after the Communion, it shall not be carried out of the Church; but the Minister and other Communicants shall, immediately after the Blessing, reverently eat and drink the same.*

¶ *If among those who come to be partakers of the Holy Communion, the Minister shall know any to be an open and notorious evil liver, or to have done any wrong to his neighbours by word or deed, so that the Congregation be thereby offended; he shall advertise him, that he presume not to come to the Lord's Table, until he have openly declared himself to have truly repented and amended his former evil life, that the Congregation may thereby be satisfied; and that he hath recompensed the parties to whom he hath done wrong; or at least declare himself to be in full purpose so to do, as soon as he conveniently may.*

¶ *The same order shall the Minister use with those, betwixt whom he perceiveth malice and hatred to reign; not suffering them to be partakers of the Lord's Table, until he know them to be reconciled. And if one of the parties, so at variance, be content to forgive from the bottom of his heart all that the other hath trespassed against him, and to make amends for that wherein he himself hath offended; and the other party will not be persuaded to a godly unity, but remain still in his frowardness and malice; the Minister in that case ought to admit the penitent person to the Holy Communion, and not him that is obstinate. Provided, That every Minister so repelling any, as is herein specified, shall be obliged to give an account of the same to the Ordinary, within fourteen days after, at the farthest.*

THE EXHORTATIONS

¶ At the time of the Celebration of the Communion, after the prayer for the whole state of Christ's Church the Priest may say this Exhortation. And NOTE, *That the Exhortation shall be said on the First Sunday in Advent, the First Sunday in Lent, and Trinity Sunday.*

DEARLY beloved in the Lord, ye who mind to come to the holy Communion of the Body and Blood of our Saviour Christ, must consider how Saint Paul exhorteth all persons diligently to try and examine themselves, before they presume to eat of that Bread, and drink of that Cup. For as the benefit is great, if with a true penitent heart and lively faith we receive that holy Sacrament; so is the danger great, if we receive the same unworthily. Judge therefore yourselves, brethren, that ye be not judged of the Lord; repent you truly for your sins past; have a lively and stedfast faith in Christ our Saviour; amend your lives, and be in perfect charity with all men; so shall ye be meet partakers of those holy mysteries. And above all things ye must give most humble and hearty thanks to God, the Father, the Son, and the Holy Ghost, for the redemption of the world by the death and passion of our Saviour Christ, both God and man; who did humble himself, even to the death upon the Cross, for us, miserable sinners, who lay in darkness and the shadow of death; that he might make us the children of God, and exalt us to everlasting life. And to the end that we should always remember the exceeding great love of our Master, and only Saviour, Jesus Christ, thus dying for us, and the innumerable benefits which by his precious blood-shedding he hath obtained for us; he hath instituted and ordained holy mysteries, as pledges of his love, and for a continual remembrance of his death, to our great and endless comfort. To him therefore, with the Father and the Holy Ghost, let us give, as we are most bounden, continual thanks; submitting ourselves wholly to his holy will and pleasure, and studying to serve him in true holiness and righteousness all the days of our life. *Amen.*

¶ When the Minister giveth warning for the Celebration of the Holy Communion, (which he shall always do upon the Sunday, or some Holy Day, immediately preceding,) he shall read this Exhortation following; or so much thereof as, in his discretion, he may think convenient.

DEARLY beloved, on —— day next I purpose, through God's assistance, to administer to all such as shall be religiously and devoutly disposed the most comfortable Sacrament of the Body and Blood of Christ; to be by them received in remembrance of his meritorious Cross and Passion; whereby alone we obtain remission of our sins, and are made partakers of the Kingdom of heaven. Wherefore it is our duty to render most humble and hearty thanks to Almighty God, our heavenly Father, for that he hath given his Son our Saviour Jesus Christ, not only to die for us, but also to be our spiritual food and sustenance in that holy Sacrament. Which being so divine and comfortable a thing to them who receive it worthily, and so dangerous to those who will presume to receive it unworthily; my duty is to exhort you, in the mean season to consider the dignity of that holy mystery, and the great peril of the unworthy receiving thereof; and so to search and examine your own consciences, and that not lightly, and after the manner of dissemblers with God; but so that ye may come holy and clean to such a heavenly Feast, in the marriage-garment required by God in holy Scripture, and be received as worthy partakers of that holy Table.

The way and means thereto is: First, to examine your lives and conversations by the rule of God's commandments; and whereinsoever ye shall perceive yourselves to have offended, either by will, word, or deed, there to bewail your own sinfulness, and to confess yourselves to Almighty God, with full purpose of amendment of life. And if ye shall perceive your offences to be such as are not only against God, but also against your neighbours; then ye shall reconcile yourselves unto them; being ready to make restitution and satisfaction, according to the uttermost of your powers, for all injuries and wrongs done by you to any other; and being likewise ready to forgive others who have offended you, as ye would have forgiveness of your offences at God's hand: for otherwise the receiving of the holy Communion doth nothing else but increase your condemnation. Therefore, if any of you be a blasphemer of God, an hinderer or slanderer of his Word, an adulterer, or be in malice, or envy, or in any other grievous crime; repent you of your sins, or else come not to that holy Table.

And because it is requisite that no man should come to the holy Communion, but with a full trust in God's mercy, and with a quiet conscience; therefore, if there be any of you, who by this means cannot quiet his own conscience herein, but requireth further comfort or counsel, let him come to me, or to some other Minister of God's Word, and open his grief; that he may receive such godly counsel and advice, as may tend to the quieting of his conscience, and the removing of all scruple and doubtfulness.

¶ *Or, in case he shall see the People negligent to come to the Holy Communion, instead of the former, he may use this Exhortation.*

DEARLY beloved brethren, on —— I intend, by God's grace, to celebrate the Lord's Supper: unto which, in God's behalf, I bid you all who are here present; and beseech you, for the Lord Jesus Christ's sake, that ye will not refuse to come thereto, being so lovingly called and bidden by God himself. Ye know how grievous and unkind a thing it is, when a man hath prepared a rich feast, decked his table with all kind of provision, so that there lacketh nothing but the guests to sit down; and yet they who are called, without any cause, most unthankfully refuse to come. Which of you in such a case would not be moved? Who would not think a great injury and wrong done unto him? Wherefore, most dearly beloved in Christ, take ye good heed, lest ye, withdrawing yourselves from this holy Supper, provoke God's indignation against you. It is an easy matter for a man to say, I will not communicate, because I am otherwise hindered with worldly business. But such excuses are not so easily accepted and allowed before God. If any man say, I am a grievous sinner, and therefore am afraid to come: wherefore then do ye not repent and amend? When God calleth you, are ye not ashamed to say ye will not come? When ye should return to God, will ye excuse yourselves, and say ye are not ready? Consider earnestly with yourselves how little such feigned excuses will avail before God. Those who refused the feast in the Gospel, because they had bought a farm, or would try their yokes of oxen, or because they were married, were not so excused, but counted unworthy of the heavenly feast. Wherefore, according to mine office, I bid you in the Name of God, I call you in Christ's behalf, I exhort you, as ye love your own salvation, that ye will be partakers of this holy Communion. And as the Son of God did vouchsafe to yield up his soul by death upon the Cross for your salvation; so it is your duty to receive the Communion in remembrance of the sacrifice of his death, as he himself hath commanded: which if ye shall neglect to do, consider with yourselves how great is your ingratitude to God, and how sore punishment hangeth over your heads for the same; when ye wilfully abstain from the Lord's Table, and separate from your brethren, who come to feed on the banquet of that most heavenly food. These things if ye earnestly consider, ye will by God's grace return to a better mind: for the obtaining whereof we shall not cease to make our humble petitions unto Almighty God, our heavenly Father.

THE SOUTH AFRICAN RITE
(1929)

'AN ALTERNATIVE FORM OF THE ORDER FOR THE ADMINISTRATION OF THE HOLY COMMUNION. SET FORTH BY AUTHORITY FOR USE IN THE CHURCH OF THE PROVINCE OF SOUTH AFRICA WHERE ALLOWED BY THE BISHOP'

THE ORDER FOR THE
ADMINISTRATION OF THE LORD'S SUPPER

OR

HOLY COMMUNION

¶ *So many as intend to be partakers of the Holy Communion shall signify their names to the Curate, at least some time the day before.*

¶ *And if any of those be living in open and unrepented sin, or in open contravention of the canonical regulations of the Church, the Curate, having knowledge thereof, shall call him and advertise him, that in any wise he presume not to come to the Lord's Table, until he have openly declared himself to have truly repented and amended his former naughty life, that the Congregation may thereby be satisfied, which before were offended; and that he have recompensed the parties, to whom he hath done wrong; or at least declare himself to be in full purpose so to do, as soon as he conveniently may.*

¶ *The same order shall the Curate use with those betwixt whom he perceiveth malice and hatred to reign; not suffering them to be partakers of the Lord's Table, until he know them to be reconciled. And if one of the parties so at variance be content to forgive from the bottom of his heart all that the other hath trespassed against him, and to make amends for that he himself hath offended; and the other party will not be persuaded to a godly unity, but remain still in his frowardness and malice: the Minister in that case ought to admit the penitent person to the Holy Communion, and not him that is obstinate. Provided that every Minister so repelling any, as is specified in this, or the next precedent paragraph of this rubrick, shall be obliged to give an account of the same to the Bishop within fourteen days after at the farthest. And, if occasion require, the Bishop shall proceed against the offending person according to the Canon.*

¶ *The Table at the Communion-time shall have a fair white linen cloth upon it. And the Priest, standing at the Table, shall say in a distinct and audible voice, the people devoutly kneeling.*

INTRODUCTION

OUR Father who art in heaven, Hallowed be thy Name, Thy kingdom come, Thy will be done, In earth as it is in heaven. Give us this day our daily bread. And forgive us our trespasses, As we forgive them that trespass against us. And lead us not into temptation; But deliver us from evil. Amen.

The Collect.

ALMIGHTY God, unto whom all hearts be open, all desires known, and from whom no secrets are hid; Cleanse the thoughts of our hearts by the inspiration of thy Holy Spirit, that we may perfectly love thee, and worthily magnify thy holy Name; through Christ our Lord. *Amen.*

¶ *Then shall the Priest, turning to the people, rehearse distinctly all the TEN COMMANDMENTS; and the people still kneeling shall, after every Commandment, ask God mercy for their transgression of every duty therein (either according to the letter or according to the spiritual import thereof) for the time past, and grace to keep the same for the time to come, as followeth.*

Minister.

I. God spake these words, and said; I am the Lord thy God: Thou shalt have none other gods but me.

II. Thou shalt not make to thyself any graven image, nor the likeness of anything that is in heaven above, or in the earth beneath, or in the water under the earth. Thou shalt not bow down to them nor worship them.

III. Thou shalt not take the Name of the Lord thy God in vain.

IV. Remember that thou keep holy the Sabbath-day. Six days shalt thou labour and do all that thou hast to do; but the seventh day is the Sabbath of the Lord thy God.

V. Honour thy father and thy mother.

VI. Thou shalt do no murder.

VII. Thou shalt not commit adultery.

VIII. Thou shalt not steal.

IX. Thou shalt not bear false witness.

¶ *And the People and Choir shall say or sing after each Commandment.*

Lord, have mercy upon us, and incline our hearts to keep this law.

X. Thou shalt not covet.

Answer. Lord, have mercy upon us, and write all these thy laws in our hearts, we beseech thee.

¶ *Provided that the* Ten Commandments *be rehearsed at least once on each Lord's Day in Advent and Lent, they may be omitted at other times. When they are so omitted, then shall follow:*

JESUS said: Thou shalt love the Lord thy God with all thy heart, and with all thy soul, and with all thy mind: This is the first and great commandment. And the second is like unto it, Thou shalt love thy neighbour as thyself. On these two commandments hang all the law and the prophets.

People. Lord, have mercy upon us, and write these thy laws in our hearts, we beseech thee.

¶ *After this summary, or instead of it, may be said or sung:*

Lord, have mercy upon us.
Christ, have mercy upon us.
Lord, have mercy upon us.

¶ *Then shall be said:*

Priest. The Lord be with you.
People. And with thy spirit.

Let us pray.

¶ *Then shall be said the Collect of the day. Other Collects, as appointed or authorised, may follow, and the last of these shall have the full ending.*

INSTRUCTION

¶ *And immediately after the Collect the Priest shall read the Epistle, saying,* The Epistle [*or,* The portion of Scripture appointed for the Epistle] is written in the —— Chapter of —— beginning at the —— Verse. *And the Epistle ended, he shall say,* Here endeth the Epistle. *Then shall he read the Gospel (the people all standing up), saying,* The holy Gospel is written in the —— Chapter of —— beginning at the —— Verse.

People. Glory be to thee, O Lord.

¶ *And after the Gospel the people shall say or sing:*

Thanks be to thee, O Lord.

¶ *And he that readeth the Epistle or Gospel shall so turn to the people that all may hear.*

I

¶ *If unbaptised or penitents be present the Sermon may here follow, after which they shall be dismissed with prayer and blessing. And then shall be sung or said the Creed following, the people all standing.*

I BELIEVE in one God the Father Almighty, Maker of heaven and earth, And of all things visible and invisible.

And in one Lord Jesus Christ, the only-begotten Son of God, Begotten of his Father before all worlds, God of God, Light of Light, Very God of very God, Begotten, not made, Being of one substance with the Father, By whom all things were made: Who for us men, and for our salvation came down from heaven, And was incarnate by the Holy Ghost of the Virgin Mary, And was made man, And was crucified also for us under Pontius Pilate. He suffered and was buried, And the third day he rose again according to the Scriptures, And ascended into heaven, And sitteth on the right hand of the Father. And he shall come again with glory to judge both the quick and the dead: Whose kingdom shall have no end.

And I believe in the Holy Ghost, The Lord, the Giver of Life, Who proceedeth from the Father and the Son, Who with the Father and the Son together is worshipped and glorified, Who spake by the Prophets. And I believe One, Holy, Catholick and Apostolick Church. I acknowledge one Baptism for the remission of sins, And I look for the Resurrection of the dead, And the life of the world to come. Amen.

¶ *Then the Curate shall declare unto the people what Feasts, or Fasting Days, are in the week following to be observed. And then also (if occasion be) shall notice be given of the Communion, and Banns of Matrimony published; and Briefs, Citations, and Excommunications read. And nothing shall be proclaimed or published in the Church, during the time of Divine Service, but by the Minister: nor by him any thing, but what is prescribed in the Rules of this Book, or enjoined by the Bishop.*

¶ *Then may follow the Sermon, unless it shall have been already preached before the Creed.*

OFFERTORY

¶ *Then shall the Priest return to the Lord's Table, and begin the Offertory, saying one or more of these Sentences following, as he thinketh most convenient in his discretion.*

ADVENT. Rejoice greatly, O daughter of Zion; shout, O daughter of Jerusalem: behold, thy King cometh unto thee.
Zechariah 9.

NATIVITY OF OUR LORD. Unto us a child is born, unto us a son is given.
Isaiah 9.

EPIPHANY. All Kings shall fall down before him; all Nations shall do him service.
Psalm 72.

LENT. Rend your hearts and not your garments, and turn unto the Lord your God: for he is gracious and merciful.
Joel 2.

PASSIONTIDE. Thy rebuke hath broken my heart; I am full of heaviness: I looked for some to have pity on me, but there was no man, neither found I any to comfort me.
Psalm 69.

EASTER. Christ is risen from the dead, and become the first-fruits of them that slept. Alleluia.   1 *Corinthians* 15.

ASCENSION. Lift up your heads, O ye gates, and be ye lift up, ye everlasting doors; and the King of Glory shall come in. Alleluia.
Psalm 24.

WHITSUNDAY. I will pour out my spirit upon all flesh. Alleluia.
Joel 2.

TRINITY. Who shall not fear thee, O Lord, and glorify thy name? for thou only art holy.
Revelation 15.

SAINTS' DAYS. All thy works praise thee, O Lord; and thy saints give thanks unto thee.
Psalm 145.

AT MEMORIALS OF THE DEPARTED. None of us liveth to himself, and no man dieth to himself. For whether we live, we live unto the Lord; and whether we die, we die unto the Lord: whether we live therefore, or die, we are the Lord's.
Romans 14.

GENERAL. Let your light so shine before men, that they may see your good works, and glorify your Father which is in heaven.
St. Matthew 5.

Lay not up for yourselves treasures upon the earth; where the rust and moth doth corrupt, and where thieves break through and steal: but lay up for yourselves treasures in heaven; where neither rust nor moth doth corrupt, and where thieves do not break through and steal. *St. Matthew* 6.

Whatsoever ye would that men should do unto you, even so do unto them; for this is the Law and the Prophets.
St. Matthew 7.

Not every one that saith unto me, Lord, Lord, shall enter into the Kingdom of heaven; but he that doeth the will of my Father which is in heaven. *St. Matthew* 7.

Remember the words of the Lord Jesus, how he said, It is more blessed to give than to receive. *Acts* 20.

Let him that is taught in the word minister unto him that teacheth, in all good things. Be not deceived, God is not mocked: for whatsoever a man soweth that shall he reap. *Galatians* 6.

While we have time, let us do good unto all men; and specially unto them that are of the household of faith.
Galatians 6.

Blessed be the man that provideth for the sick and needy: the Lord shall deliver him in the time of trouble. *Psalm* 41.

Walk in love, as Christ also hath loved us, and hath given himself for us an offering and a sacrifice to God, for a sweet smelling savour. *Ephesians* 5.

I beseech you therefore, brethren, by the mercies of God, that ye present your bodies a living sacrifice, holy, acceptable unto God, which is your reasonable service. *Romans* 12.

Melchizedek King of Salem brought forth bread and wine; and he was the Priest of the most high God. *Genesis* 14.

I will offer to thee the sacrifice of thanksgiving, and will call upon the Name of the Lord; I will pay my vows unto the Lord in the sight of all his people. *Psalm* 116.

All things come of thee, and of thine own have we given thee. 1 *Chronicles* 29.

¶ *Whilst these Sentences are in reading, the Deacons, Churchwardens, or other fit person appointed for that purpose, shall receive the Alms and other offerings of the people, in a decent bason to be provided by the Parish for that purpose; and reverently bring it to the Priest, who shall humbly present and place it upon the Holy Table.*

¶ *And the Priest shall place upon the Table so much Bread and Wine, as he shall think sufficient, saying:*

BLESS, O Lord, we beseech thee, these thy gifts and sanctify them unto this holy use, that by them we may be fed unto everlasting life of soul and body; through Jesus Christ our Lord. *Amen.*

¶ *When Intercession or Thanksgiving is to be offered for any special object, it shall be provided for by a Form of Bidding either here or before the Offertory.*

After which done, the Priest shall say,

Let us pray for the whole state of Christ's Church.

ALMIGHTY and everliving God, who by thy holy Apostle hast taught us to make prayers, and supplications, and to give thanks, for all men; We humbly beseech thee most mercifully to accept our (*alms and*) oblations and to receive these our prayers, which we offer unto thy Divine Majesty; beseeching thee to inspire continually the universal Church with the spirit of truth, unity and concord: And grant, that all they that do confess thy holy Name may agree in the truth of thy holy Word, and live in unity, and godly love.

We beseech thee also to lead all nations into the way of righteousness and peace, and to direct all Kings, Presidents and Rulers that under them the world may be godly and quietly governed. And grant unto thy Servant George our King, his ministers and parliaments, and all that are set in authority throughout his Dominions, that they may truly and impartially minister justice to the removing of wickedness and vice, and to the maintenance of order and right living.

Give grace, O heavenly Father, to all Bishops, Priests and Deacons, and especially to thy Servant N. our Bishop, that they may both by their life and doctrine set forth thy true and living Word, and rightly and duly administer thy

117

holy Sacraments: And to all thy people give thy heavenly grace; and specially to this congregation here present; that, with meek heart and due reverence, they may hear, and receive thy holy Word; truly serving thee in holiness and righteousness all the days of their life. [Guide and prosper, we pray thee, all those who are labouring for the spread of thy Gospel among the nations.]

[And to all Schools and Universities grant the light of thy Spirit, that the world may be filled with the knowledge of thy Truth.] [And grant to all men in their several callings that they may seek the common welfare, and promote good will and brotherhood on earth.]

And we most humbly beseech thee of thy goodness, O Lord, to comfort and succour all them, who in this transitory life are in trouble, sorrow, need, sickness, or any other adversity.

And we commend to thy gracious keeping, O Lord, all thy servants departed this life in thy faith and fear, beseeching thee to grant them mercy, light and peace both now and at the day of resurrection.

And here we do give unto thee, O Lord, most high praise and hearty thanks for the wonderful grace and virtue declared in all thy Saints, and chiefly in the Blessed Virgin Mary, Mother of thy Son Jesus Christ, our Lord and God, and in the holy Patriarchs, Prophets, Apostles and Martyrs; beseeching thee to give us grace that we, rejoicing in the Communion of the Saints, and following the good examples of those who have served thee here, may be partakers with them of thy heavenly kingdom:

Grant this, O Father, for Jesus Christ's sake, our only Mediator and Advocate. *Amen.*

PREPARATION

¶ *Then shall the Priest say to them that come to receive the Holy Communion,*

YE that do truly and earnestly repent you of your sins, and are in love and charity with your neighbours, and intend to lead a new life, following the commandments of God, and walking from henceforth in his holy ways; Draw near with faith, and take this holy Sacrament to your comfort; and make your humble confession to Almighty God, meekly kneeling upon your knees.

¶ *Then shall this general Confession be made, in the name of all those that are minded to receive the Holy Communion, by one of the Ministers; both he and all the people kneeling humbly upon their knees, and saying,*

ALMIGHTY God, Father of our Lord Jesus Christ, Maker of all things, Judge of all men; We acknowledge and bewail our manifold sins and wickedness, Which we, from time to time, most grievously have committed, By thought, word, and deed, Against thy Divine Majesty, Provoking most justly thy wrath and indignation against us. We do earnestly repent, And are heartily sorry for these our misdoings; The remembrance of them is grievous unto us; The burden of them is intolerable. Have mercy upon us, Have mercy upon us, most merciful Father; For thy Son our Lord Jesus Christ's sake, Forgive us all that is past; And grant that we may ever hereafter Serve and please thee In newness of life, To the honour and glory of thy Name; Through Jesus Christ our Lord. Amen.

¶ *On working days, not being Feasts, with the permission of the Bishop, the following shortened form of Confession and Absolution may be used:*

Priest and People. We confess to God Almighty, the Father, the Son, and the Holy Ghost, that we have sinned in thought, word, and deed, through our own grievous fault. Wherefore we pray God to have mercy upon us.

¶ *Then shall the Priest (or the Bishop, being present) stand up, and turning himself to the people, pronounce this Absolution.*

ALMIGHTY God, our heavenly Father, who of his great mercy hath promised forgiveness of sins to all them that with hearty repentance and true faith turn unto him; Have mercy upon you; pardon and deliver you from all your sins; confirm and strengthen you in all goodness; and bring you to everlasting life; through Jesus Christ our Lord. *Amen.*

Priest. Almighty God have mercy upon you, forgive you all your sins, and deliver you from all evil, confirm and strengthen you in all goodness, and bring you to everlasting life. *Amen.*

¶ *Then shall the Priest say,*

Hear what comfortable words our Saviour Christ saith unto all that truly turn to him.

COME unto me all that travail and are heavy laden, and I will refresh you. *St. Matthew* 11. 28.

So God loved the world, that he gave his only-begotten Son, to the end that all that believe in him should not perish, but have everlasting life. *St. John* 3. 16.

Hear also what Saint Paul saith.

This is a true saying, and worthy of all men to be received, That Christ Jesus came into the world to save sinners.

1 *Timothy* 1. 15.

Hear also what Saint John saith.

If any man sin, we have an Advocate with the Father, Jesus Christ the righteous; and he is the propitiation for our sins. 1 *St. John* 2. 1.

CONSECRATION

¶ *When the Priest, standing before the Table, hath so ordered the Bread and Wine, that he may with the more readiness and decency break the Bread before the people, and take the Cup into his hands, he shall say the Prayer of Consecration, as followeth.*

Priest.   The Lord be with you.
Answer.   And with thy spirit.
Priest.   Lift up your hearts.
Answer.   We lift them up unto the Lord.
Priest.   Let us give thanks unto our Lord God.
Answer.   It is meet and right so to do.

¶ *Then shall the Priest turn to the Lord's Table, and say,*

IT is very meet, right, and our bounden duty, that we should at all times, and in all places, give thanks unto thee, O Lord, Holy Father, Almighty, Everlasting God.

¶ *Here shall follow the Proper Preface (see pages 128 to 130) according to the time, if there be any specially appointed: or else shall follow on Sundays,*

WHO with thine only begotten Son and the Holy Ghost art one God, one Lord, in Trinity of Persons and in Unity of Substance, who hast created all things through thy eternal Word. Therefore with Angels, &c.

¶ *On other days shall follow immediately:*

THEREFORE with Angels and Archangels and with all the company of heaven, we laud and magnify thy glorious Name; evermore praising thee, and saying:
　Holy, holy, holy, Lord God of hosts, heaven and earth are full of thy glory: Glory be to thee, O Lord most high. Amen.

ALL Glory and Thanksgiving be to thee, Almighty God, our heavenly Father, for that thou of thy tender mercy didst give thine only Son Jesus Christ to take our nature upon him, and to suffer death upon the cross for our redemption; who (by his one oblation of himself once offered) made a full, perfect, and sufficient sacrifice, oblation, and satisfaction, for the sins of the whole world; and did institute, and in his holy Gospel command us to continue, a perpetual memory of that his precious death, until his coming again.

Hear us, O merciful Father, we most humbly beseech thee; and grant that we, receiving these thy creatures of bread and wine, according to thy Son our Saviour Jesus Christ's holy institution, in remembrance of his death and passion, may be partakers of his most blessed Body and Blood: who, in the same night that he was betrayed, *took bread; and, when he had given thanks, †he brake it, and gave it to his disciples, saying, Take, eat, ‡this is my Body which is given for you: Do this in remembrance of me. Likewise after supper he ||took the Cup; and, when he had given thanks, he gave it to them, saying, Drink ye all of this; for this §is my Blood of the New Testament, which is shed for you and for many for the remission of sins: Do this, as oft as ye shall drink it, in remembrance of me.

* Here the Priest is to take the Paten into his hands:

† And here to break the Bread:

‡ And here to lay his hand upon all the Bread:

|| Here he is to take the Cup into his hand:

§ And here to lay his hand upon every vessel (be it Chalice or Flagon) in which there is any Wine to be consecrated.

Wherefore, O Lord and heavenly Father, according to the institution of thy dearly beloved Son, our Saviour Jesus Christ, we thy humble servants, having in remembrance his blessed passion and precious death, his mighty resurrection and glorious ascension, do render unto thee most hearty thanks for the innumerable benefits procured unto us by the same; and, looking for his coming again with power and great glory, we offer here unto thy divine majesty this holy Bread of eternal life and this Cup of everlasting salvation; and we humbly beseech thee to pour thy Holy Spirit upon us and upon these thy gifts, that all we who are partakers of this holy Communion may worthily receive the most precious Body and Blood of thy Son, and be fulfilled with thy grace and heavenly benediction.

And we entirely desire thy fatherly goodness mercifully

to accept this our sacrifice of praise and thanksgiving; most humbly beseeching thee to grant that, by the merits and death of thy Son Jesus Christ, and through faith in his blood, we and all thy whole Church may obtain remission of our sins, and all other benefits of his passion.

And here we offer and present unto thee, O Lord, ourselves, our souls and bodies, to be a reasonable, holy, and living sacrifice unto thee.

And although we be unworthy, through our manifold sins, to offer unto thee any sacrifice, yet we beseech thee to accept this our bounden duty and service; not weighing our merits, but pardoning our offences, through Jesus Christ our Lord; by whom, and with whom, in the unity of the Holy Ghost, all honour and glory be unto thee, O Father Almighty, world without end.

¶ *Here let all the people say:* Amen.

As our Saviour Jesus Christ hath commanded and taught us, we are bold to say:

¶ *Then shall the Priest and People say together the Lord's Prayer.*

OUR Father, who art in heaven, Hallowed be thy Name, Thy kingdom come, Thy will be done, In earth as it is in heaven. Give us this day our daily bread. And forgive us our trespasses, As we forgive them that trespass against us. And lead us not into temptation; But deliver us from evil.

For thine is the kingdom, The power, and the glory, For ever and ever. Amen.

COMMUNION

¶ *Then shall silence be kept for a space, after which shall follow this prayer, said by the Priest, kneeling, in the name of all them that shall receive the Communion.*

WE do not presume to come to this thy Table, O merciful Lord, trusting in our own righteousness, but in thy manifold and great mercies. We are not worthy so much as to gather up the crumbs under thy Table. But thou art the same Lord, whose property is always to have mercy: Grant us therefore, gracious Lord, so to eat the flesh of thy dear Son Jesus Christ, and to drink his blood, that our sinful bodies may be made clean by his body, and our souls washed through his most precious blood, and that we may evermore dwell in him, and he in us. *Amen.*

¶ *Then shall the Priest break the Bread, and first receive the Communion in both kinds himself, and then proceed to deliver the same to the Bishops, Priests, and Deacons, in like manner, (if any be present,) and after that to the people also in order, into their hands, all meekly kneeling. And, when he delivereth the Bread to any one, he shall say,*

THE Body of our Lord Jesus Christ, which was given for thee, preserve thy body and soul unto everlasting life. Take and eat this in remembrance that Christ died for thee, and feed on him in thy heart by faith with thanksgiving.

¶ *And the Minister that delivereth the Cup to any one shall say,*

THE Blood of our Lord Jesus Christ, which was shed for thee, preserve thy body and soul unto everlasting life. Drink this in remembrance that Christ's Blood was shed for thee, and be thankful.

¶ *Or else the Priest shall, before he delivereth the Bread to the people, say to the whole Congregation,*

DRAW near and receive the Body and Blood of our Lord Jesus Christ, which were given for you, and feed on him in your hearts by faith with thanksgiving.

¶ *And if he have so said, when he delivereth the Bread to any one, he shall say,*

THE Body of our Lord Jesus Christ preserve thy body and soul unto everlasting life.

¶ *And the Minister that delivereth the Cup to any one shall say,*

THE Blood of our Lord Jesus Christ preserve thy body and soul unto everlasting life.

¶ *When all have communicated, the Priest shall return to the Lord's Table, and reverently place upon it what remaineth of the consecrated Elements, covering the same with a fair linen cloth; or else, at his discretion, reverently consume the same.*

THANKSGIVING

¶ Then shall he say this Thanksgiving for Communion.

Priest.   O give thanks unto the Lord, for he is gracious.
Answer.   And his mercy endureth for ever.

ALMIGHTY and everliving God, we most heartily thank
thee, for that thou dost vouchsafe to feed us, who have
duly received these holy mysteries, with the spiritual food
of the most precious Body and Blood of thy Son our Saviour
Jesus Christ; and dost assure us thereby of thy favour and
goodness towards us; and that we are very members incorporate in the mystical body of thy Son, which is the blessed
company of all faithful people; and are also heirs through
hope of thy everlasting kingdom, by the merits of the most
precious death and passion of thy dear Son. And we most
humbly beseech thee, O heavenly Father, so to assist us
with thy grace, that we may continue in that holy fellowship, and do all such good works as thou hast prepared for
us to walk in; through Jesus Christ our Lord, to whom, with
thee and the Holy Ghost, be all honour and glory, world
without end. *Amen.*

¶ Then shall be said or sung,

GLORY be to God on high, and in earth peace, good
will towards men. We praise thee, we bless thee, we
worship thee, we glorify thee, we give thanks to thee for thy
great glory, O Lord God, heavenly King, God the Father
Almighty.
   O Lord, the only-begotten Son Jesu Christ; O Lord God,
Lamb of God, Son of the Father, that takest away the sins
of the world, have mercy upon us. Thou that takest away the
sins of the world, have mercy upon us. Thou that takest away
the sins of the world, receive our prayer. Thou that sittest
at the right hand of God the Father, have mercy upon us.
   For thou only art holy; thou only art the Lord; thou only,
O Christ, with the Holy Ghost, art most high in the glory
of God the Father. Amen.

¶ Then the Priest (or the Bishop, if he be present) shall let them depart with this Blessing.

THE peace of God, which passeth all understanding, keep your hearts and minds in the knowledge and love of God, and of his Son Jesus Christ our Lord: and the blessing of God Almighty, the Father, the Son, and the Holy Ghost, be amongst you and remain with you always. *Amen.*

¶ Collects which may be said after the Collect of the Day, or before the Blessing. Other Collects may also be sanctioned by the Bishop as need require.

LOOK with favour, most Holy Trinity, on this our act of worship and service; and may this sacrifice set forth before thine eyes be acceptable to thy Divine Majesty, and avail for us and all for whom we have offered it, who livest and reignest, one God, world without end. *Amen.*

O LORD Jesus Christ, who didst say to thine Apostles, Peace I leave with you, my peace I give unto you; regard not our sins but the faith of thy Church, and grant it that peace and unity which is agreeable to thy will; who livest and reignest with the Father and the Holy Spirit, one God, world without end. *Amen.*

O ETERNAL Lord God, who holdest all souls in life; We beseech thee to shed forth upon thy whole Church in Paradise and on earth the bright beams of thy light and heavenly comfort; and grant that we, following the good example of those who have loved and served thee here and are now at rest, may with them at length enter into the fulness of thine unending joy; through Jesus Christ our Lord. *Amen.*

ASSIST us mercifully, O Lord, in these our supplications and prayers, and dispose the way of thy servants towards the attainment of everlasting salvation; that, among all the changes and chances of this mortal life, they may ever be defended by thy most gracious and ready help; through Jesus Christ our Lord. *Amen.*

O ALMIGHTY Lord, and everlasting God, vouchsafe, we beseech thee, to direct, sanctify, and govern, both our hearts and bodies, in the ways of thy laws, and in the works of thy commandments; that through thy most mighty protection, both here and ever, we may be preserved in body and soul; through our Lord and Saviour Jesus Christ. *Amen.*

GRANT, we beseech thee, Almighty God, that the words, which we have heard this day with our outward ears, may through thy grace be so grafted inwardly in our hearts, that they may bring forth in us the fruit of good living, to the honour and praise of thy Name; through Jesus Christ our Lord. *Amen.*

PREVENT us, O Lord, in all our doings with thy most gracious favour, and further us with thy continual help; that in all our works begun, continued and ended in thee, we may glorify thy holy Name, and finally by thy mercy obtain everlasting life; through Jesus Christ our Lord. *Amen.*

ALMIGHTY God, the fountain of all wisdom, who knowest our necessities before we ask, and our ignorance in asking; We beseech thee to have compassion upon our infirmities; and those things, which for our unworthiness we dare not, and for our blindness we cannot ask, vouchsafe to give us, for the worthiness of thy Son Jesus Christ our Lord. *Amen.*

ALMIGHTY God, who hast promised to hear the petitions of them that ask in thy Son's Name; We beseech thee mercifully to incline thine ears to us that have made now our prayers and supplications unto thee; and grant, that those things, which we have faithfully asked according to thy will, may effectually be obtained, to the relief of our necessity, and to the setting forth of thy glory; through Jesus Christ our Lord. *Amen.*

PROPER PREFACES

Upon Christmas-day, *and until* the Epiphany, *and* (*the words* 'as at this time' *being omitted*) *on* the Feasts of the Purification and the Annunciation.

BECAUSE thou didst give Jesus Christ thine only Son to be born as at this time for us; who, by the operation of the Holy Ghost, was made very man of the substance of the Virgin Mary his mother; and that without spot of sin, to make us clean from all sin. Therefore with Angels, &c.

Upon the Epiphany *and seven days after.*

THROUGH Jesus Christ our Lord; who, in substance of our mortal flesh, manifested forth his glory, that he might bring all men everywhere out of darkness into his own marvellous light. Therefore with Angels, &c.

Upon Thursday before Easter.

THROUGH Jesus Christ our Lord; who, having loved his own which were in the world, loved them unto the end, and on the night before he suffered did institute these holy mysteries, that we receiving the benefits of his Passion, and being quickened by his Resurrection, might be made partakers of his divine nature, and be filled with all the fulness of God. Therefore with Angels, &c.

Upon Easter-day *and until* Ascension-day.

BUT chiefly are we bound to praise thee for the glorious Resurrection of thy Son Jesus Christ our Lord: for he is the very Paschal Lamb, which was offered for us, and hath taken away the sin of the world; who by his death hath destroyed death, and by his rising to life again hath restored to us everlasting life. Therefore with Angels, &c.

Upon Ascension-day *and until* Whit-sunday.

THROUGH thy most dearly beloved Son Jesus Christ our Lord; who after his most glorious Resurrection manifestly appeared to all his Apostles, and in their sight ascended up into heaven to prepare a place for us; that where he is, thither we might also ascend, and reign with him in glory. Therefore with Angels, &c.

Upon Whit-sunday *and six days after.*

THROUGH Jesus Christ our Lord; who, after that he had ascended up far above all the heavens and was set down at the right hand of thy Majesty, did as at this time pour forth upon the children of adoption thy holy and life-giving Spirit, that through his glorious power the joy of the everlasting gospel might go forth into all the world; whereby we have been brought out of darkness and error into the clear light and true knowledge of thee, and of thy Son our Saviour Jesus Christ. Therefore with Angels, &c.

Upon Trinity Sunday.

WHO with thine only-begotten Son and the Holy Ghost art one God, one Lord, in Trinity of Persons and in Unity of Substance; for that which we believe of thy glory, O Father, the same we believe of the Son and of the Holy Ghost, without any difference or inequality. Therefore with Angels, &c.

Upon the Transfiguration.

BECAUSE the glory of thine Incarnate Word did shine forth upon the holy mount unto eyewitnesses of his Majesty, and did manifest the power and coming of his Kingdom with his Saints in light. Therefore with Angels, &c.

Upon All Saints' Day, *and* (*except when the Proper Preface of any of the Great Festivals is appointed to be said*) *upon the Festivals of* Apostles and Evangelists, *and* the Nativity of St. John Baptist.

WHO in thy Saints hast given us an example of godly life and a glorious pledge of the hope of our calling; that, compassed about with so great a cloud of witnesses, we may run with patience the race that is set before us, and receive with them the crown of glory that fadeth not away. Therefore with Angels, &c.

At Memorials of the Departed.

THROUGH Jesus Christ our Lord; who hath brought life and immortality to light, that we, who are burdened by the weight of sin and death, may grieve not as those who have no hope; because we know that when our earthly tabernacle is dissolved we have a better habitation. Therefore with Angels, &c.

Upon the Dedication of a Church, *or* Anniversary of the Dedication.

WHO, though the Heaven of heavens cannot contain thee, and thy glory is in all the world, yet dost accept the earthly habitations dedicated to thy name, and in them dost pour forth gifts of grace upon thy faithful people. Therefore with Angels, &c.

¶ *When the Minister giveth warning for the celebration of the Holy Communion, he shall, at the least before the Great Festivals, and at other times according to his discretion, read this Exhortation following.*

DEARLY beloved, on —— day next I purpose, through God's assistance, to administer to all such as shall be religiously and devoutly disposed the most comfortable Sacrament of the Body and Blood of Christ; to be by them received in remembrance of his meritorious Cross and Passion; whereby alone we obtain remission of our sins, and are made partakers of the kingdom of heaven.

Wherefore it is our duty to render most humble and hearty thanks to Almighty God our heavenly Father, for that he hath given his Son our Saviour Jesus Christ, not only to die for us, but also to be our spiritual life and sustenance in that holy Sacrament; unto which, in God's behalf, I bid you all that are here present, who are so lovingly called and bidden by God himself; and I exhort you, as ye love your own salvation, that ye will be partakers of this holy Communion.

It is an easy matter for a man to say, I will not communicate, because I am otherwise hindered with worldly business. But such excuses are not so easily accepted and allowed before God. And if any man say, I am a grievous sinner, and therefore am afraid to come: wherefore then do ye not repent and amend? I beseech you, therefore, for the Lord Jesus Christ's sake, that ye will not refuse to come to this holy Sacrament, in which we spiritually eat the flesh of Christ, and drink his Blood; in which we dwell in Christ, and Christ in us; we are one with Christ, and Christ with us.

And, because we must receive these holy mysteries with a penitent heart and living faith, it is my duty in the mean-time to exhort you to remember the dignity of that holy mystery, and to consider how Saint Paul exhorteth all persons diligently to examine themselves, before they presume to eat of that Bread, and drink of that Cup. Judge therefore yourselves, brethren, that ye be not judged of the Lord; examine yourselves by the rule of God's commandments; have a living and stedfast faith in Christ our Saviour; amend your lives, and be in perfect charity with all men; so shall ye be meet partakers of those holy mysteries.

And if ye shall perceive your offences to be such as are not only against God, but also against your neighbours, then ye shall reconcile yourselves unto them; being ready to make restitution and satisfaction, according to the uttermost of your powers, for all injuries and wrongs done by you to any other; and being likewise ready to forgive others that have offended you, as ye would have forgiveness of your offences at God's hand.

And because it is requisite, that no man should come to the holy Communion, but with a full trust in God's mercy, and with a quiet conscience; therefore if there be any of you, who by this means cannot quiet his own conscience herein, but requireth further comfort or counsel, let him come to me, or to some other Minister of God's Word, and open his grief; that by the ministry of God's holy Word he may receive the benefit of absolution, together with spiritual counsel and advice, to the quieting of his conscience, and avoiding of all scruple and doubtfulness.

¶ *And there shall be no celebration of the Lord's Supper, except there be at least one to communicate with the Priest.*

¶ *And in Cathedral and Collegiate Churches, and Colleges, where there are many Priests and Deacons, they shall all receive the Communion with the Priest every Sunday at least, except they have a reasonable cause to the contrary.*

¶ *And to take away all occasion of dissension, and superstition, which any person hath or might have concerning the Bread and Wine, it shall suffice that the Bread be such as is usual to be eaten; but the best and purest Wheat Bread that conveniently may be gotten.*

¶ *If the Consecrated Bread or Wine be spent before all have communicated the Priest is to consecrate more, either* (a) *in both kinds, repeating the Words of the Consecration Prayer beginning 'Hear us, O Merciful Father' and ending at 'heavenly benediction'; or* (b) *in either kind, according to the Form given for this purpose in the Book of Common Prayer.*

¶ *And if any remain of the Bread and Wine which was consecrated, it shall not be carried out of the Church, but the Priest and such other of the Communicants as he shall then call unto him shall, immediately after the Blessing, reverently eat and drink the same: except so far as is otherwise provided in the Order for the Communion of the Sick.*[1]

¶ *The Bread and Wine for the Communion shall be provided by the Curate and the Churchwardens at the charges of the Parish.*

¶ *It is the duty of every Communicant to receive the Holy Sacrament frequently, and especially at all the Great Festivals of the Church, of which Easter to be one. The canonical obligation of a Communicant of the Church of this Province is to receive the Holy Communion three times at least during the year.*

¶ *And yearly at Easter every Parishioner shall reckon with the Parson, Vicar, or Curate, or his or their Deputy or Deputies; and pay to them or him all Ecclesiastical Duties, accustomably due, then and at that time to be paid.*

¶ *After the Divine Service ended, the money given at the Offertory shall be disposed of to such pious and charitable uses, as the Minister and Churchwardens shall think fit. Wherein if they disagree, it shall be disposed of as the Ordinary shall appoint.*

¶ *On working days, not being Feasts, with the permission of the Bishop, the Creed and Gloria in Excelsis may be omitted, and the shortened form of Confession and Absolution may be used* (pp. 119 and 120).

---

[1] The 'Order for the Communion of the Sick' to which this rubric refers, is contained in *An Alternative Form of the Calendar and Offices of the Church* (1936), and provides as follows:

But if the sick person, desirous to receive the Holy Communion in his house, does not wish that the service be celebrated there, or if it cannot be there celebrated reverently or conveniently, as also when there are several sick persons in the Parish desirous to receive the Holy Communion on the same day, the Curate shall administer the reserved Sacrament in such form and manner as shall be sanctioned by the Bishop.

THE INDIAN LITURGY
(1933)

AN ORDER FOR THE ADMINISTRATION OF THE
HOLY COMMUNION SANCTIONED IN 1922 BY
THE EPISCOPAL SYNOD OF INDIA FOR EX-
PERIMENTAL USE IN THE DIOCESE OF BOMBAY
IN PLACES SELECTED BY THE BISHOP OF
BOMBAY; AND IN 1933 GIVEN PROVINCIAL
AUTHORISATION (I.E. FOR USE IN ANY
DIOCESE OF THE CHURCH OF INDIA, BURMA,
AND CEYLON, IN WHICH THE BISHOP
CHOOSES TO SANCTION IT)

THE LITURGY

THE PREPARATION SERVICE

*Every celebration of the Holy Communion shall be preceded by a service of preparation, at which all those who purpose to communicate shall as of obligation be present. This service shall ordinarily be held on some day preceding the celebration; but where this is for any reason impossible or undesirable, it may be held immediately before the celebration commences. The Office of Preparation shall include some time for quiet self-examination, in which matter the Priest may give direction to the thoughts of his people by questions based upon the Ten Commandments or the twofold Law of Love, or by any other such questions as may seem to him most convenient for bringing them to a lively sense of their sins. And thereafter they shall all together make confession of the same, and receive assurance of absolution, for which purpose the Priest may at his discretion use the form of Confession, Absolution, and the Comfortable Words, as contained in the English Prayer Book of 1662, following the same with the Prayer beginning:—*We do not presume to come to this thy Table, O merciful Lord, *and with such other prayers, elsewhere contained or of his own creating, as he may deem fit.*

THE LITURGY

THE PRAYERS BEFORE THE SERVICE

Before the service, the Deacon shall set in readiness so much bread upon the Paten, and so much wine, mixed with a little pure water, in the Chalice, as he shall think sufficient; and the Priest shall bless them, saying the prayer following:

O LORD our God, who didst send forth thy heavenly Bread, the food of the whole world, even Jesus Christ thine only Son, to save us and to redeem us, to bless us and to sanctify us: Vouchsafe now to ble✠ss this our oblation, and to accept it on thine altar in Heaven. Do thou remember, O Lover of Man, both them that offer it and them for whom it is offered; and do thou preserve us thy servants uncondemned in the ministration of the divine mysteries: for hallowed and blessed is thy glorious name, O Father, Son, and Holy Spirit, now and ever, and world without end. Amen.

Then shall the Deacon set the sacred vessels upon the altar, covering them with a decent veil.

And, at the time appointed, being duly vested, the Priest and all those who are to share in the service of the sanctuary, standing in the vestry, shall say the prayers following:

Priest. Peace be with you.

Answer. And with thy spirit.

Priest. Glory be to the Father, and to the Son, and to the Holy Ghost.

Answer. As it was in the beginning, is now, and ever shall be: world without end. Amen.

Priest. Let us pray.

ALMIGHTY and all-holy Father, we thine unworthy servants humbly entreat thy Majesty so to prepare us for this sacred service, that entering with a pure heart into thy sanctuary, we may offer to thee the sacrifice of this Holy Eucharist for thy honour and glory; in remembrance of thy manifold mercies vouchsafed to us in our Saviour Jesus Christ; for the well-being of thy whole Church; and to the remission of our own manifold sins and offences. Vouchsafe, O Fountain of Mercy, to accept this our pure sacrifice through the merits of Jesus Christ our Saviour; who liveth and reigneth with thee and the Holy Spirit, ever One God, world without end. Amen.

THE PRAYERS OF THE CATECHUMENS

During the entry of the Priest and his attendants into the church, shall be sung the Introit, which at Christmas, Easter, and all other Great Festivals shall be as follows:

G LORY to God in the highest, and upon earth peace, good hope unto men. We praise thee; we bless thee; we worship thee; the fulness of glory do we offer thee; we give thanks to thee for thy great glory, O Lord our Maker, heavenly King, God the Father Almighty: and to thee, O Lord, the only-begotten Son, Jesu Christ, with the Holy Ghost.

O Lord God, Lamb of God, Son and Word of the Father, that bearest now, as once thou didst bear, the sin of the world, have mercy upon us. Thou that bearest now, as once thou didst bear, the sin of the world, incline thine ear and hear our prayer. Thou that sittest in glory at the right hand of the Father, shew thy pity and have mercy upon us.

For thou only art holy, thou only art the Lord, O Jesu Christ, with the Holy Ghost, in the glory of God the Father. Amen.

[*The Introit ended, the Priest, having set on incense and blessed it, shall solemnly cense the altar and sanctuary therewith, after which the Deacon, taking the censer from him, shall cense the celebrant and other ministers and persons in the sanctuary, as also the choir, congregation, and the whole church, the people standing.*

And, at the time when he censes the altar, the Priest shall say:

May the incense of the merits of Christ our Saviour which we plead before thee, O Lord our God, avail unto us for the remission of our sins and for the reward of eternal life; and do thou, O life-giving Son, who by thy Cross hast saved us, set us on thy right hand in the day when thy mercy dawneth; who livest and reignest God for ever and ever.

And the people shall answer here, and after all other prayers which the Priest says with a loud voice, Amen.]*   * *Where incense is not used, the portions within brackets may be omitted.*

Then the Deacon shall say the Litany, which shall always include at least these biddings here following: and if there be any other matters, concerning which thanksgiving or prayer is to be offered, they shall be inserted after that bidding with which they shall appear most consonant.

After each several bidding to thanksgiving the people shall answer:

Thanks be to God;

and after each bidding to prayer:

Lord, have mercy.

Let us thank God for his manifold mercies vouchsafed unto us.

Let us pray for Christian people, specially for those in this diocese.

Let us pray for the healing of the divisions of Christendom.

Let us pray for the peace of the whole world.

Let us pray for missionary workers, and for God's blessing upon their labours.

Let us pray for catechumens and inquirers.

Let us pray for the conversion of all unbelievers.

Let us pray for the coming of God's kingdom in this world.

Let us pray for preservation from sickness, pestilence and famine.

Let us pray for the supply of all our manifold necessities.

Let us pray for all in need, sickness, or suffering.

Let us pray for the faithful departed.

The Priest, meantime, standing in the sanctuary with his attendants, shall make silent intercession to Almighty God; and, the Litany ended, he shall say this collect following:

O LORD, who hast given us grace with one accord to make our common supplications unto thee, and dost promise, that if two or three shall be agreed together in thy name thou wilt grant their requests; fulfil now the desires and petitions of thy servants, as may be most expedient for them; granting us in this world knowledge of thy truth, and in the world to come life everlasting. Amen.

Priest. Peace be with you.
People. And with thy spirit.
Priest. Let us pray.

Then shall be said the Collect of the Day.

And, immediately after the Collect, the people being seated, a Deacon, or other fit person appointed for the purpose, shall read the Lesson from the Old Testament, saying:

The Lesson is written in the —— Chapter of —— beginning at the —— verse. *And, the Lesson ended, he shall say,* Here endeth the Lesson.

Then shall a Psalm or portion of a Psalm be sung.

Then shall the Deacon read the Epistle, saying:

The Epistle is written in the —— Chapter of —— beginning at the —— verse. *And, the Epistle ended, he shall say,* Here endeth the Epistle.

Then shall be sung an hymn, the people standing. And, during this singing, the Priest shall say privately:

Grant us, O Lord God, the knowledge of thy divine words, and fill us with the understanding of thy holy gospel; that we may in all things fulfil thy blessed will, and be accounted worthy of the merits which proceed from thee, now and for ever. Amen.

[*Then shall he again set on and bless the incense, which shall be burned during the reading of the Gospel.*]

Then shall the Deacon say:

In silence stand and give heed unto the Holy Gospel.

And the Priest shall read the Gospel, saying first:

Peace be with you.
People. And with thy spirit.
Priest. The Holy Gospel is written in the —— Chapter of —— beginning at the —— verse.
People. Glory be to thee, O Lord.

And after the Gospel, they shall say:

Thanks be to thee, O Christ.

Then shall the Priest, or other minister, declare unto the people what holy-days, or fasting days, are in the week following to be observed. He shall publish banns of marriage, and shall inform the people of all matters concerning which notice is needed to be given.

Then shall follow the Sermon or Instruction.

And, the Sermon ended, the churchwardens shall receive the alms and other devotions of the people, and shall bring them to the Deacon, who shall say:

Let us pray for them that bring an offering,

the people making answer:

Accept the offering of the brethren, accept the offering of the sisters, accept the offering of us all.

Then shall the Deacon bring the alms and devotions to the Priest, who shall present them before God at the altar, saying this prayer following:

WE beseech thee, Almighty Lord, for them that bring an offering within thy one holy Catholic Church, an oblation, first fruits, a thank-offering, a vow, in secret or openly, whether much or little; and for them that desire but have not wherewith to give. Accept the ready mind of all, and grant them thy blessing both now and always.

Then shall the Deacon say:

Let us pray unto God for the catechumens, that he may reveal unto them the gospel of truth, and may unite them unto his holy Church.

And the Priest shall say:

O LORD our God, who dwellest in the heavens, and lookest in mercy upon all thy works; look down upon thy servants, the catechumens, who have bowed their heads before thee; grant them gladly to bear thine easy yoke, and make them to be members of thy holy Church; account them worthy of the washing of regeneration for the remission of their sins, and clothe them in the incorruptible garment of thy salvation, that they may know thee, the only true God, and may with us exalt thy mighty and all-glorious name, with the name of thy blessed Son, and of thy Holy Spirit, now and ever, and world without end. Amen.

Then shall the Deacon give notice to the catechumens and to all unbaptized or excommunicate persons that they forthwith depart from the church, saying:

Let all catechumens now depart.

Let none that is excommunicate or unbaptized remain in the church.

And he shall take good heed that none remain.

But if there be no catechumens present, the Prayer for the Catechumens together with the Deacon's bidding and the Dismissal shall be omitted.

THE PRAYERS OF THE FAITHFUL

Then the people standing, the Deacon shall say:

Let us who are of the household of faith together make profession of our Christian belief, and say:

The Priest and the people. I believe in one God the Father Almighty, Maker of heaven and earth, and of all things visible and invisible:

And in one Lord Jesus Christ, the only-begotten Son of God, Begotten of his Father before all worlds, God of God, Light of Light, Very God of very God, Begotten, not made, Being of one substance with the Father, By whom all things were made: Who for us men, and for our salvation, came down from heaven, And was incarnate by the Holy Ghost of the Virgin Mary, And was made man, And was crucified also for us under Pontius Pilate. He suffered and was buried, And the third day he rose again according to the Scriptures, And ascended into heaven, And sitteth on the right hand of the Father, And he shall come again with glory to judge both the quick and the dead: Whose kingdom shall have no end.

And I believe in the Holy Ghost, the Lord, and the Giver of life, Who proceedeth from the Father and the Son, Who with the Father and the Son together is worshipped and glorified, Who spake by the Prophets. And I believe one holy Catholic and Apostolic Church. I acknowledge one Baptism for the remission of sins. And I look for the Resurrection of the dead, and the life of the world to come. Amen.

Then shall the Deacon say:

Give we the Peace.

The Priest. Grant, O Lord, that free from all guile and hypocrisy, we may greet one another with an holy kiss.

And, turning to the people, he shall say:

The peace of the Lord be always with you.

And they shall answer:

And with thy spirit.

Then shall the Peace be given.

And, in the meanwhile, a basin of water being brought to him, the Priest shall wash his hands therein, saying privately:

WASH away, O Lord God, the foul pollution of my soul, and cleanse me with the water of life; that in all purity and holiness I may be accounted worthy to enter thy holy of holies.

Then shall he remove the veil from the sacred vessels, saying privately:

O GOD our Father, who of thy tender love towards mankind didst send thy Son into the world to bring back the sheep that had gone astray: reject not us who offer unto thee this bloodless sacrifice, for we trust not in our own righteousness but in thy mercies, and grant that this mystery which is administered for our salvation be not turned to our condemnation; but that we may thereby receive remission of our sins, and may render unto thee due praise and thanksgiving; as also unto thine only-begotten Son, and to thine all-holy and quickening Spirit, now and ever, and world without end. Amen.

[And thereafter shall he cense the oblation, saying:

WE offer unto thee incense, O Lord our God, for a savour of spiritual sweetness; beseeching thee to accept it before thine altar in heaven, and to send down upon us the grace of thy Holy Spirit, now and ever. Amen.]

THE ANAPHORA

Then the Priest, turning to the people, shall say:

THE love of God the Fa✠ther; the grace of the only-begotten S✠on; and the fellowship and indwelling of the Holy Spi✠rit be with you all, my brethren, for ever.

The people. And with thy spirit.

The Priest. Your hearts be with Christ on high.
The people. Our hearts are with the Lord.

The Priest. Let us give thanks unto our Lord God.
The people. It is meet and right so to do.

And, turning again to the Altar, the Priest shall proceed, saying:

It is very meet, right, and our bounden duty, that we should at all times, and in all places, give thanks unto thee, O holy Lord, Father Almighty, Everlasting God.

Here shall follow the Proper Preface according to the season. After each of which Prefaces shall be said:

Therefore with martyrs and apostles, and with the great company of thy saints triumphant, we laud and magnify thy glorious Name: and we worship and adore thy Majesty with angels and archangels, and with all the host of heaven, who ever fly before thy throne, praising thee, and chanting, and saying,

The people. Holy, holy, holy, Lord God of hosts, heaven and earth are full of thy glory. Glory be to Thee, O Lord most high.

[*And here it is to be noted, that from the singing of* Holy, Holy, Holy, *until the end of the Great Intercession, incense is to be burned within the Sanctuary.*]

Then shall the Priest proceed, saying:

HOLY in truth art thou, O Father Almighty, Eternal King, and in thine every gift and work dost thou reveal thy holiness unto men. Holy is thine only-begotten Son, our Saviour, Jesus Christ, by whom thou framedst the worlds; and holy thine ever-blessed Spirit, who searcheth out thy secret things.

Even as in truth thou art holy, O Lord, so also that he might dwell in holiness before thee, didst thou create man in thine own image; whom, when he transgressed thy commandments and fell, thou didst not abandon nor despise, but didst chasten him as a merciful Father, speaking unto him by thy priests and by thy prophets; and, when the fulness of time was come, thou spakest unto us also by thine only-begotten Son, whom thou didst send into the world to take our nature upon him, that he might become man like as we are, and might renew thine image within us;

Who, in the same night that he gave himself to suffer death upon the Cross for our redemption, took bread into his holy and spotless hands, and, looking heavenward unto thee (*here the Priest is to look upward*), O God our Father, bless✠ed, brake, and gave it to his apostles, saying: Take, eat; this is my Body which is given for you for the remission of sins and for life everlasting.

And the people shall say: Amen.

Likewise after supper he took the cup, and, when he had given thanks, he bless✠ed and gave it to them, saying: Drink ye all of this; for this is my Blood of the New Testament, which is shed for you, and for many, for the remission of sins and for life everlasting.

And again the people shall say: Amen.

Do this in remembrance of me; for as oft as ye eat this bread and drink this cup, ye do show forth my death and proclaim my resurrection until I come.

The people. Thy death, O Lord, we commemorate; thy resurrection we confess; and thy second coming we await. We ask of thee, also, mercy and compassion, and implore forgiveness of our sins.

And the Priest shall proceed, saying:

Wherefore, O heavenly Father, we thine humble servants, being mindful of the precious death of thy Son, our Saviour, Jesus Christ; as also of his glorious resurrection from the dead; his triumphant ascension into heaven; and his session in majesty at thy right hand; do offer unto thee this our reasonable service and sacrifice, making with these thy creatures of bread and wine the memorial which thy Son hath willed us to make, and rendering unto thee most hearty thanks for all thy dispensation towards us.

The people. We give thanks to thee, we praise thee, we glorify thee, O Lord our God, and we pray thee to show thy mercy upon us and to hearken unto the voice of our prayer.

Then the Deacon shall give warning to the people, saying:

How solemn, O my brethren, is this time, wherein we implore the holy and quickening Spirit to descend and hallow this our Eucharist. Let us fall and worship in holy fear.

And therewith they shall all fall prostrate with their faces to the ground, and shall so continue till the Great Intercession be ended. And, the people being thus prostrate, the Priest shall say the Invocation of the Holy Spirit:

SHEW us thy mercy, we pray thee, O Lord, and upon us and upon these gifts here set before thee send down thy Holy Spirit, that by his power this bread and this wine may become unto us the Bo✠dy and the Bl✠ood of thy Son, our Saviour Jesus Christ, and may hallow the spirits, the souls, and the bodies of all who partake of them, to the bringing forth of the fruit of good works and to the strengthening of thy Church upon the rock of faith; through the same Jesus Christ, thy Son, our Lord, to whom with thee and the Holy Spirit be all honour and glory, world without end. Amen.

Then shall silence be kept for a space, the people worshipping.

And thereafter the Deacon, standing and turning to the people, shall say:

Let us pray unto the Lord for his grace and mercy.

Let us pray for the whole state of Christ's Church.

Let us pray, at this dread time, for all men both living and departed.

L

And the Priest shall proceed with the Great Intercession, saying:

O ALMIGHTY Lord God and Maker of all things, whose blessed Son, by his death upon the Cross, made one, perfect, and sufficient sacrifice for all mankind, that with boldness they might draw nigh unto the throne of grace and find acceptance in his name: receive our supplications and prayers, which through him we now offer unto thy Majesty; making intercession before all things for thy holy Church throughout the world, and entreating thee to endue her with the gifts of thy Holy Spirit and to grant unto her that peace and unity which are agreeable to thy will.

The people. Amen.

And therein we pray for all Bishops, Priests, Deacons, and other orders of thy Church, and specially for *NN*; beseeching thee to grant them thy grace, that both by their life and doctrine they may set forth thy true and lively Word, and rightly and duly fulfil the ministry which thou hast committed to their charge. Amen.

And we humbly beseech thee, O Lord, to remember for good all them that travel by land, by water, or by air; as also to be mindful of them that suffer oppression, captivity, bondage, want, sickness, or any other adversity; and to show thy pity upon them that are vexed by unclean spirits. Send unto them the angel of thy mercy to comfort and relieve them according to their several necessities, and to preserve them to the attainment of eternal life. Amen.

To us also thy servants, O Lord, and to all thy Christian people, vouchsafe thy grace and thy mercy; that we may be preserved from all things hurtful both to our souls and bodies, and may be delivered from those afflictions which through our sins are fallen upon us. Grant us to continue in the true faith of thy holy Church, and to walk steadfastly in the ways of thy commandments unto our lives' end. Amen.

We pray thee also, O Lord, to remember all Christian governors and those in authority under them, specially *NN*; aid them with the armour of thy Spirit, that in all things they may seek thy honour and glory, and that under them thy people may joyfully serve thee in all quietness and godly fear. Amen.

And we entreat thee also, O Lord, mercifully to bless the air and the dews, the rains and the winds; that through thy heavenly benediction we may be saved from dearth and famine, and may enjoy the fruits of the earth in all abundance and plenty; for the eyes of all wait upon thee, O Lord, and thou givest them their meat in due season. Amen.

And here, O heavenly Father, we yield unto thee praise and thanksgiving for thy great glory declared in thy saints from the beginning of the world, but specially in the glorious and ever-blessed Virgin Mary, Mother of Jesus Christ, our Lord and God, as also in thy holy Apostle Saint Thomas (*and, if it be the Feast-day of any other saint or saints, or confessor or martyr, here shall be added:* Thy blessed Saint *N*, or Saints *NN*, or thy blessed Confessor *N*, or Martyr *N*), and in all thine evangelists and doctors, who have been thy witnesses unto the uttermost parts of the earth; and we beseech thee so to unite us to their holy fellowship that they may share with us in the communion of this our Eucharist and continually assist us by their prayers. Amen.

Finally, we commend to thy fatherly goodness the souls of thy servants who have departed hence from us with the sign of faith, and now repose in the sleep of peace. Grant unto them, we beseech thee, O Lord, thy tender mercy and everlasting rest.

The people. Rest eternal grant unto them, O Lord, and let light perpetual shine upon them.

The Priest. And vouchsafe unto us their brethren an end both Christian and free from sin, and gather us beneath the feet of thine elect, when thou wilt and as thou wilt, only without shame by reason of our faults; that in this, as in all things, thy blessed Name may be exalted and glorified together with the Name of our Lord Jesus Christ and of thine all-holy and quickening Spirit, now and ever, and world without end. Amen.

Then shall the Priest perform the Fraction, saying privately:

Grant, we beseech thee, merciful Lord, that, as the body of thy blessed Son was broken (*here the Priest shall break the Host*) on the Cross (*here the Priest shall make the sign of the Cross over the chalice with a portion of the broken Host*) that we might become one with him; so we who now partake of these holy mysteries may be united in the fellowship of his mystical Body and (*here the Priest shall place the portion of the Host in the chalice*) share with him in the glory of his resurrection; through the same Jesus Christ our Lord. Amen.

And, if the number of those desiring to communicate be large, the Deacon shall assist the Priest in breaking the bread.

And while the Priest performs the Fraction the people shall in the meantime sing the anthem following:

We have known the Lord, Alleluia: in the breaking of the bread, Alleluia.

The bread which we break, Alleluia: is the Body of our Lord Jesus Christ, Alleluia.

The cup which we bless, Alleluia: is the Blood of our Lord Jesus Christ, Alleluia.

And the anthem ended, the Priest shall say:

As our Saviour Christ hath commanded and taught us, we are bold to say:

And all together shall say:

Our Father, which art in heaven, Hallowed be thy Name, Thy kingdom come, Thy will be done, in earth as it is in heaven. Give us this day our daily bread; And forgive us our trespasses, As we forgive them that trespass against us; And lead us not into temptation, But deliver us from evil.

And the Priest shall proceed:

Yea, Lord, we pray thee, suffer us not to be tempted above that we are able, but deliver us from the power of the evil one: for thine is the kingdom, the power, and the glory, for ever and ever. Amen.

The Priest. Peace be with you.
The people. And with thy spirit.

Then shall the Deacon say:

Let us pray unto the Lord that he make us worthy to partake of these his holy mysteries.

And the Priest shall say the following prayer:

Grant us thy blessing, we beseech thee, O Lord; and of thy mercy vouchsafe that in all purity of heart and mind we may receive the Communion of the Body and Blood of thy Son: who with thee and the Holy Spirit liveth and reigneth for ever. Amen.

And turning himself to the people, he (or the Bishop, if he be present) shall bless them, saying:

May the mer✠cy of our God and Saviour Jesus Christ be with you all, my brethren, for ever.

Then shall the Deacon say: Give we heed in fear.

And the Priest, extending the Gifts towards the people, shall say:

Holy things for holy persons.

And the people shall answer:

Blessed is he that cometh in the name of the Lord. Hosanna in the highest.

Then shall he first receive the Gifts in both kinds himself, saying when he partaketh of the bread: The Body of Christ, the Bread of Life;

and, when he partaketh of the cup:

The Blood of Christ, the Chalice of Life;

and to whomsoever the Gifts be administered, these same words shall be used therewith.

And thereafter he shall deliver the same to such of the Deacons and other persons within the sanctuary and of the choir, as shall be minded to partake of the Holy Communion. And afterwards the people shall receive thereof, as they may be disposed.

And to the words of administration, both of the bread and of the cup, the communicant shall answer, Amen.

And during the administration of the Holy Sacrament to the people shall be sung:

O Lamb of God, that takest away the sins of the world; have mercy upon us.

O Lamb of God, that takest away the sins of the world; have mercy upon us.

O Lamb of God, that takest away the sins of the world; grant us thy peace.

Or some other hymn.

And, when all have communicated, the Priest shall return to the altar, and shall reverently consume what remaineth of the Consecrated Elements (except such as he may wish to reserve for the Communion of the sick), and thereafter he shall cleanse the sacred vessels after the usual manner, and again cover them with the veil.

And, turning to the people, he shall say: Peace be with you.

And they shall answer: And with thy spirit.

Then shall the Deacon say:

Let us give thanks unto the Lord, for that he hath vouchsafed us to partake of his holy mysteries, and hath refreshed us with food from his heavenly table.

And the people shall answer:

Thanks be to him for his unspeakable gift.

Then shall the Priest say this prayer following:

MERCIFUL Father, who of thine abundant goodness towards us hast vouchsafed to feed and strengthen us with the precious body and blood of thy Son our Saviour Jesus Christ, and dost thereby make us one with him and with all the members of his mystical body, and dost enable us in the power of that sacred communion to overcome sin and to walk as children of light; for these thy bountiful mercies we most heartily thank thee, we praise and worship thee. And we beseech thee to give us grace so to continue in that holy fellowship, that we may ever walk in the steps of thy blessed Son, and offer ourselves a living sacrifice acceptable unto thee; through the same Jesus Christ our Lord, to whom, with thee and thy quickening Spirit, be ascribed, as is most justly due, all praise and thanksgiving now and ever, and world without end. Amen.

Then shall the people and the choir sing this hymn following:

STRENGTHEN, Lord, for holy service hands which took thy
mysteries here;
Be the ears which heard thy praises shielded from the voice
of fear;
Eyes which saw thy great compassion see thy blessed hope
appear.

May the tongues which chanted 'Holy' ever unto truth
incline;
Grant the feet which walked thy temple in the land of light
to shine;
Bodies, by thy Body nourished, quicken thou with life
divine.

With thy worshippers abide thou; may thy love direct our
ways;
Hear the prayers we lift before thee, and accept our thankful
praise.
May thy peace and mercy keep us safe from harm through
all our days.

In the hour of thine appearing may we stand before thy
face;
Raise we ever glad hosannas for the wonder of thy grace;
For thy love hath shined upon us to redeem our mortal race.

Lord, who deign'st on our offences mercy's pardoning
streams to pour,
Grant us grace to own thy God-head and in reverent faith
adore,
To thy sovereignty uplifting praise and blessing evermore.
Amen.

Or this:

FROM glory unto glory advancing on our way,
We hymn thee, Christ our Saviour, our soul's eternal stay.

From strength to strength advancing, as from thy house
we go,
We pray thee in our weakness thy perfect strength to show.

Direct our way before thee; preserve us in thy love;
And grant us through thy mercy thy heavenly realm above.

From glory unto glory advancing on our way,
We hymn thee, Christ our Saviour, our soul's eternal stay.

Or this; when the service is not sung:

FINISHED and perfected is the mystery of thy dispensation, as far as in us lies. We have made the memorial
of thy Death, we have seen the symbol of thy Resurrection,
we have been filled with thine inexhaustible bounty, and
enriched with thine undying life; of the which do thou
vouchsafe to count us worthy in the world to come, O
Christ our God; to whom with thy Father eternal and thine
all-holy and quickening Spirit be ascribed, as is most justly
due, all praise and thanksgiving, now and ever, and world
without end. Amen.

Then the Priest, turning to the people, shall let them go, saying:

Unto the mercies of the holy and glorious Trinity, brethren, we commit you; go ye with the food of your pilgrimage
in pea✠ce and gladness.

*And, the people being thus dismissed, the Priest and those with him in the sanctuary
shall forthwith return to the vestry.*

THE VESTRY PRAYERS

The Priest, having returned to the vestry, shall say:

O LORD, who hast vouchsafed unto us to be sanctified
by the participation of the most holy Body and
precious Blood of thine only-begotten Son Jesus Christ our
Lord, grant us also the grace of thy Holy Spirit, that we
may be preserved unblameable in the faith, and lead us
unto our perfect sonship and redemption, and to the attainment of everlasting felicity; who with the same thine only-
begotten Son and thine all-holy Spirit art our sanctification
and light, now and always. Amen.

Then shall the Deacon say:

Be we preserved in the peace of Christ.

The Priest. Blessed be God, who blesseth and sanctifieth us by the receiving of his holy and spotless mysteries, now and for ever, and world without end. Amen.

THE PROPER PREFACES TO BE USED THROUGHOUT THE YEAR

On Trinity Sunday, *and all the Sundays of the year for which no Proper Preface has been appointed:*

WHO with thine only-begotten Son and the Holy Spirit art one God and one Lord; not one only Person, but three Persons in one substance, for that which by thy revelation we believe of thy glory, the same we believe of thy Son and of the Holy Spirit, without any difference or inequality. Therefore with martyrs, *&c.*

From the first Sunday in Advent *until* Christmas Eve, *save when the Proper Preface for any Saint's Day is appointed to be said:*

THROUGH Jesus Christ our Lord; who, at his first coming into the world in fashion as a man, did promise in the form of God to come again with glory, that he might receive his people into the place which he had prepared for them, and that as kings they might reign with him for ever. Therefore, *&c.*

From Christmas Day, *until* Epiphany:

BECAUSE thou didst give Jesus Christ, thine only Son, to be born as on this day (*but between Christmas Day and Epiphany shall be said:* as at this time) for us; who by the operation of the Holy Ghost, was made very Man, of the substance of the blessed Virgin Mary his Mother, and that without spot of sin, to make us clean from all sin. Therefore with martyrs, *&c.*

Upon the Epiphany *and seven days after:*

THROUGH Jesus Christ our Lord, who, in substance of our mortal flesh, manifested forth his glory, that he might bring us out of darkness into his marvellous light. Therefore, *&c.*

Upon the Purification, *as also upon the* Commemoration of the blessed Sacrament, *and Feast of the* Holy Name:

BECAUSE, through the mystery of the Incarnate Word, the new light of thy brightness has shone upon our understanding, that while we acknowledge him to be the visible God, we may be raised up by him to the love of things invisible. Therefore, *&c.*

Upon the Annunciation, *and all other feasts of the* Blessed Virgin Mary *save the Purification:*

BECAUSE thou didst give Jesus Christ, thine only Son, to be born for us; who, by the operation of the Holy Ghost, was made very Man, of the substance of the blessed Virgin Mary his Mother, and that without spot of sin to make us clean from all sin. Therefore, *&c.*

Another Preface which may be used on all feasts of the Blessed Virgin Mary *save the Purification:*

BECAUSE by the overshadowing of the Holy Ghost the blessed and ever-glorious Virgin Mary did both conceive thine only-begotten Son, and in the glory of her virginity pour forth the eternal light upon the world, even Jesus Christ our God. Therefore, *&c.*

From Ash Wednesday *until the* Saturday before Passion Sunday, *save when any other Proper Preface is appointed to be said:*

THROUGH Jesus Christ our Lord; who for our sakes did as at this time fast forty days and forty nights, and was in all points tempted like as we are, yet without sin, to the intent that we, which are tempted, may, through him, come boldly to the throne of grace, that we may obtain mercy and find grace to help in time of need. Therefore, *&c.*

From Passion Sunday *till* Maundy Thursday:

THROUGH Jesus Christ our Lord; who, being found in fashion as a man, humbled himself and became obedient unto death, even the death of the Cross, that, being lifted up from the earth, he might draw all men unto him. Therefore, &c.

Upon Easter Day *and seven days after; and from the Monday following the first Sunday after Easter until the Ascension Day, save when any other Proper Preface is appointed to be said:*

BUT chiefly are we bound to praise thee for the glorious Resurrection of thy Son Jesus Christ our Lord, for he is the very Paschal Lamb which was offered for us, and hath taken away the sin of the world; who by his death hath destroyed death, and by his rising to life again hath restored to us everlasting life. Therefore, &c.

From Ascension Day *till* Whitsun Eve, *save when the Proper Preface for any Saint's Day is appointed to be said:*

THROUGH thy most dearly beloved Son Jesus Christ our Lord; who, after his most glorious Resurrection, manifestly appeared to all his Apostles, and in their sight ascended up into heaven to prepare a place for us; that where he is, thither we might also ascend, and reign with him in glory. Therefore, &c.

Upon Whitsunday, *and six days after:*

THROUGH Jesus Christ our Lord; who ascending up into heaven and sitting on thy right hand, according to his most true promise did as on this day (*during the six days after Whitsunday shall be said:* as at this time) send down thine Holy Spirit upon the children of adoption, to teach them and to lead them into all truth, giving them boldness with fervent zeal constantly to preach the Gospel unto all nations; whereby we have been brought out of darkness and error into the clear light and true knowledge of thee, and of thy Son Jesus Christ. Therefore, &c.

Upon Feasts of Apostles *and* Evangelists, *save when the Proper Preface for any of the Great Festivals is appointed to be said:*

THROUGH Jesus Christ our Lord; who did vouchsafe to choose thy servant, Saint *N* (*or* thy servants Saint *N* and Saint *N*) to be of the company of the Apostles (*or* to be an Evangelist), by whose ministry thine elect might be gathered in from every nation, and thy Church instructed in the way that leadeth unto everlasting life. Therefore, *&c.*

Upon All Saints' Day, *and all other Saints' Days for which no Proper Preface is appointed to be said:*

WHO in the multitude of thy Saints hast compassed us about with so great a cloud of witnesses, to the end that we, rejoicing in their fellowship, may run with patience the race that is set before us, and together with them receive the crown of glory that fadeth not away. Therefore, *&c.*

At the Dedication *of a Church, and upon the Anniversary of the Dedication:*

WHO in temples made with hands buildest up for thyself a spiritual temple made without hands. Therefore, *&c.*

At the Consecration of Bishops, *and at the* Ordination of Priests and Deacons:

THROUGH Jesus Christ our Lord, the great Shepherd of the sheep, who, for the feeding and guidance of his flock, did appoint divers orders of ministers in his Church. Therefore, *&c.*

At the Commemoration of the Departed:

THROUGH Jesus Christ our Lord, in whom there hath shined forth on us the hope of a blessed resurrection, that we who are grieved with the certain knowledge of our mortality may by the firm assurance of immortality be comforted; seeing that in death thy faithful servants die not, though they be changed; for when the house of their earthly tabernacle is dissolved, there is prepared for them an habitation eternal in the heavens. Therefore, *&c.*

APPENDIX I

[Comprises Collects to be used upon certain feasts and upon several other occasions.]

APPENDIX II

THE CENSING AND THE KISS OF PEACE

It is contrary to Anglican tradition, and, owing to architectural arrangements, frequently impossible, that ceremonies should be 'in all places one'. It is, however, desirable that the Censing and the Kiss of Peace should be everywhere the same.

I. *The Censing.*—This is not done after the Western fashion. The celebrant takes the censer (the chains of which are not usually more than two feet in length) in his right hand, and standing several paces away from the front of the altar, bows and censes the middle of it three times. He next censes the north and south ends. Going then to the north side, he censes there, and proceeding to the south side and censing as he goes, he censes the south side of the sanctuary. The deacon then takes the censer from him, and censes the celebrant three times. He then censes each person in the sanctuary in the same way, and going into the body of the church, censes the congregation on either side of the central aisle.

II. *The Kiss of Peace, or 'Shāntiwandan'.*[1]—The deacon takes the chains of the censer just above the lid into his left hand, and in his right holds them at the top. He then approaches the altar to the right of the celebrant, and kissing it, presents the centre of the hanging chains. The celebrant takes the centre of the chains into his right hand, and kissing them, offers his hand to the deacon to kiss. The deacon kisses it, and the priest makes the sign of the cross on his (the deacon's) forehead. He then relinquishes his hold of the chains, and the deacon, again kissing the altar, goes to the bishop and other priests in the sanctuary, if any be present, and receives from them the kiss in the same way. Still holding the chains as described above, the deacon next approaches any other deacon or deacons in the sanctuary, and turning his palms inwards takes the right hand of the other between them, and so receives the kiss from him. Finally, relinquishing his hold of the

[1] Literally 'Salutation of Peace'.

chains above the lid, he holds the censer in his right hand only, and going to the nearest layman of the congregation, takes the layman's outstretched right hand between his joined palms, and so gives him the kiss. The layman passes the kiss to his neighbour in the same way, and he to his, and so on until all in the church have received it.

APPENDIX III

A SHORTENED FORM FOR WEEK-DAY CELEBRATIONS

For obvious reasons it would be impossible to use the Liturgy in its present form for week-day celebrations. For this purpose it would need to be considerably shortened, and at the same time would need to be a service complete in itself. We would, therefore, suggest that only the following should be used:

   i. The Litany and the Prayer after it, 'O Lord, who hast given us grace'.

   ii. The Collect.

   iii. The Epistle.

   iv. The Gospel, and the Prayer before the Gospel.

   v. The Creed.

   vi. The Lavatory Prayer, 'Wash away, O Lord God'. [Could be omitted, if considered unnecessary.]

   vii. The Prayer of the Veil, 'O God our Father, who of Thy tender love'.

   viii. The whole of the Anaphora, from 'The Love of God the Father' to the Prayer of Thanksgiving, omitting 'We have known the Lord', &c., and 'O Lamb of God', &c.

   ix. The third hymn before the Dismissal 'Finished and Perfected', said by the people.

   x. The Dismissal.

The celebrant himself should say the diaconal biddings, unless assisted by a deacon. Should it be necessary, the biddings for the dismissal of the catechumens, excommunicate, or unbaptized should be said; but the preceding prayer should be omitted.

THE CEYLON LITURGY
(1938)

'AN ORDER FOR THE ADMINISTRATION OF THE HOLY COMMUNION SANCTIONED BY THE EPISCOPAL SYNOD FOR USE IN THE DIOCESE OF COLOMBO SUBJECT TO THE PROVISIONS OF CANON XIV OF CHAPTER XXI OF THE CONSTITUTION, CANONS, AND RULES OF THE CHURCH OF INDIA, BURMA, AND CEYLON'

THE CEYLON LITURGY

GENERAL RUBRICS

1. *The Deacon's part may be taken by any ordained Minister. In the absence of an ordained Minister to assist at the Service, the Priest shall say the portions assigned to the Deacon.*

2. *Note that whenever the Salutation* The Lord be with you *is said, or the Epistle or Gospel is read, or other words are spoken to the people, then the Minister shall so stand and turn himself as he may best be heard of the people.*

3. *It is convenient, however, that the Priest (in the absence of an ordained Minister to assist him) in saying the Biddings before the Confession, the Creed, or the Thanksgiving say the same facing the Altar.*

4. *It is customary for the Priest to stand at the midst of the Altar for the Kyries, the Gloria in Excelsis, the Creed, the Offertory, the Offertory Prayer, and the Consecration; and at the south side of the Altar for the Collect or Collects at the Introduction and for the prayers after Communion.*

5. *It shall be permissible to say or sing the Kyries in the ancient form as follows:*

Kyrie, eleison.
Kyrie, eleison.
Kyrie, eleison.

Christe, eleison.
Christe, eleison.
Christe, eleison.

Kyrie, eleison
Kyrie, eleison.
Kyrie, eleison.

6. *If more than one Collect be said, it is customary for the Priest to say* Let us pray *at the beginning of the first and second Collects only. Only the first and the last Collects are said with full endings.*

   If a Collect be addressed to God the Father, it should conclude Through Jesus Christ thy Son our Lord, who liveth and reigneth with thee in the unity of the Holy Ghost, ever one God, world without end. Amen.

   If a Collect be addressed to God the Son, it should conclude Who livest and reignest with the Father, in the unity of the Holy Ghost, ever one God, world without end. Amen.

   If mention of God the Son be already made in the body of a Collect, the Collect should conclude Through the same thy Son, Jesus Christ, our Lord, who liveth and reigneth with thee in the unity of the Holy Ghost, ever one God, world without end. Amen.

If mention of God the Holy Spirit be already made in the body of a Collect, the Collect should conclude Through Jesus Christ thy Son our Lord, who liveth and reigneth with thee in the unity of the same Spirit, ever one God, world without end. Amen.

7. *At a Requiem, the Service may be concluded after the Post-Communion prayers as follows:*

Priest. The Lord be with you;
Answer. And with thy spirit.
Priest. May they rest in peace;
Answer. Amen.

8. *In cases where conscientious difficulty is felt on the part of any Priest or Congregation to the use of the words* beseeching thee to grant them mercy, everlasting light, and peace *in the Offertory Prayer, the Bishop may use his authority to allow their omission.*

9. *It shall be permissible for the Priest at his discretion to substitute the words of administration either as appointed in the Book of Common Prayer or as permitted in the Prayer Book as proposed in 1928 in place of the words prescribed in this Order.*

10. *It shall be permissible for the Priest at his discretion to take the ablutions immediately after the Blessing. In which case, the Priest and those with him in the sanctuary shall return to the sacristy immediately after the ablutions.*

11. *If the ablutions are to be taken after the Blessing, the Priest shall return to the Altar when all have communicated and shall reverently place upon it what remaineth of the consecrated Elements, covering the same with a fair linen cloth.*

A DEVOTION

which may be said by the Priest with the ministers present either in the sacristy or at the foot of the Altar immediately before the Introduction.

When it is said at the foot of the Altar, the Priest may say it either with the ministers present or with the ministers and with the people.

Priest. In the name of the Father, and of the Son, and of the Holy Ghost. Amen.

Anthem. I will go unto the altar of God: even unto the God of my joy and gladness.

(*Here follows* Psalm 43, Judica me Deus, with Gloria Patri.)

Anthem. I will go unto the altar of God: even unto the God of my joy and gladness.

Priest. Our help standeth in the name of the Lord;
Answer. Who hath made heaven and earth.

When this Devotion is said in the sacristy, the Priest may add a suitable prayer here.

THE CEYLON LITURGY

AN ORDER FOR THE ADMINISTRATION OF THE
HOLY COMMUNION

THE INTRODUCTION

During the entry of the Priest and his attendants a Psalm or Hymn may be sung.
When there is an Introit, the Devotion, if it is to be said by the Priest and people, will immediately follow the Introit.
The Priest standing at the foot of the Altar shall say:

Let us pray.

ALMIGHTY God, unto whom all hearts be open, all desires known, and from whom no secrets are hid: Cleanse the thoughts of our hearts by the inspiration of thy Holy Spirit, that we may perfectly love thee, and worthily magnify thy holy name; through Christ our Lord. *Amen.*

Then shall the following Confession be said by the Priest and people together, all kneeling, the Deacon first saying:

Let us make humble confession of our sins to God.

WE confess to God Almighty, the Father, the Son, and the Holy Ghost, that we have sinned in thought, word, and deed, through our own grievous fault. Wherefore we pray God to have mercy upon us.

ALMIGHTY God, have mercy upon us, forgive us all our sins and deliver us from all evil, confirm and strengthen us in all goodness, and bring us to life everlasting; through Jesus Christ our Lord. Amen.

And the Priest (or the Bishop being present) standing up and turning to the people shall say:

MAY the Almighty and merciful Lord grant unto you pardon and remission of all your sins, time for amendment of life, and the grace and comfort of the Holy Spirit. *Amen.*

The following shall then be sung or said, the Priest standing at the Altar:

Lord, have mercy.
Lord, have mercy.
Lord, have mercy.

Christ, have mercy.
Christ, have mercy.
Christ, have mercy.

Lord, have mercy.
Lord, have mercy.
Lord, have mercy.

On Sundays (except in Advent, and on the Sundays from Septuagesima to Palm Sunday inclusive) and other Greater Feasts throughout the year the Gloria in Excelsis may be said or sung here. [See pp. 173 and 182.]

When it is omitted in this place, it is to be said or sung before the Blessing on Sundays (except in Advent, and on the Sundays from Septuagesima to Palm Sunday inclusive) and other Greater Feasts throughout the year.

Then shall the Priest say:

The Lord be with you.
Answer. And with thy spirit.
Priest. Let us pray.

Then shall be said the Collect of the Day.

Other Collects, as appointed or authorized, may follow, and the last of these shall have the full ending.

THE MINISTRY OF THE WORD

Immediately thereafter he that readeth the Epistle (the people being seated) shall say: The Epistle [*or* The Lesson] is written in the —— chapter of ——, beginning at the —— verse. *And the reading ended, he shall say:* Here endeth the Epistle [*or* the Lesson].

A Psalm or a portion of a Psalm or a Hymn may be sung here.

Then the Deacon or Priest that readeth the Gospel (the people all standing up) shall say:

The Lord be with you.
Answer. And with thy spirit.

Deacon or Priest. The Holy Gospel is written in the —— chapter of the Gospel according to Saint ——, beginning at the —— verse.

Answer. Glory be to thee, O Lord.

The Gospel ended, there may be said:

Praise be to thee, O Christ.

Alleluia *may be added to the responses before and after the Gospel from Easter Day until Trinity Sunday inclusive.* ◦

On Sundays and other Greater Feasts shall then be sung or said the Creed following, the people all standing and the Deacon first saying:

Let us make profession of our Christian belief.

I BELIEVE in one God the Father Almighty, Maker of heaven and earth, And of all things visible and invisible: And in one Lord Jesus Christ, the only-begotten Son of God, Begotten of his Father before all worlds, God of God, Light of Light, Very God of very God, Begotten, not made, Being of one substance with the Father, By whom all things were made: Who for us men, and for our salvation came down from heaven, And was incarnate by the Holy Ghost of the Virgin Mary, And was made man, And was crucified also for us under Pontius Pilate. He suffered and was buried, And the third day he rose again according to the Scriptures, And ascended into heaven, And sitteth on the right hand of the Father. And he shall come again with glory to judge both the quick and the dead: Whose kingdom shall have no end.

And I believe in the Holy Ghost, The Lord, The Giver of life, Who proceedeth from the Father and the Son, Who with the Father and the Son together is worshipped and glorified, Who spake by the Prophets.

And I believe One Holy Catholic and Apostolic Church. I acknowledge one Baptism for the remission of sins. And I look for the Resurrection of the dead, And the Life of the world to come. Amen.

Notices may be given out here.

Biddings for special thanksgiving and prayer may be made here by the Deacon. In making the biddings to thanksgiving and prayer, the Deacon may stand on the chancel step facing the people, the people all standing.

A Sermon or Instruction may follow here.

THE OFFERTORY

Then the Priest, turning to the people, shall say:

BELOVED, let us love one another: for love is of God.

And turning again to the Altar, the Priest shall begin the Offertory saying one or more of the Sentences following, or the Priest and Clerks shall sing the same.

OFFER unto God the sacrifice of thanksgiving; and pay thy vows unto the Most High. *Psalm* 50. 14.

I will offer in his dwelling an oblation with great gladness: I will sing, and speak praises unto the Lord. *Psalm* 27. 7.

I beseech you, brethren, by the mercies of God, to present your bodies a living sacrifice, holy, acceptable to God, which is your reasonable service. *Romans* 12. 1.

I will offer to thee the sacrifice of thanksgiving: and will call upon the name of the Lord. *Psalm* 116. 15.

Melchizedek king of Salem brought forth bread and wine: and he was priest of God Most High. *Genesis* 14. 18.

Whoso hath the world's goods, and beholdeth his brother in need, and shutteth up his compassion from him, how doth the love of God abide in him? 1 *St. John* 3. 17.

Let him that is taught in the Word communicate unto him that teacheth in all good things. *Galatians* 6. 6.

Additional Sentences for special occasions are set forth at the end of this Order, on pp. 175-177.

The Priest shall then place upon the Holy Table so much Bread and Wine mingled with a little pure water, as he shall think sufficient, whilst the alms and other devotions of the people are received.

During this a Psalm or Hymn may be sung.

When the alms and other devotions of the people have been presented before God by the Priest, he shall say the prayer that followeth, first saying:

[*For the alternative see p.* 180.]

Let us pray.

WE humbly beseech thee, O Father, most mercifully to accept these our (alms and) oblations which we offer unto thy Divine Majesty; through Jesus Christ our Lord. *Amen.*

Then shall the Deacon standing begin the Litany following, which may be sung or said:

ALMIGHTY God, who hast taught us to make prayers, supplications, and intercessions for all men; hear us when we pray:

That it may please thee to inspire continually the universal Church with the spirit of truth, unity, and concord;

Hear us, we beseech thee.

That it may please thee to grant that all they that do confess thy holy name may agree in the truth of thy holy Word, and live in unity and godly love;

Hear us, we beseech thee.

That it may please thee to lead all nations in the paths of righteousness and peace;

Hear us, we beseech thee.

That it may please thee to direct all kings and rulers, especially thy servant *George,* our King, that under them the world may be godly and quietly governed;

Hear us, we beseech thee.

That it may please thee to give grace to all Bishops, Priests, and Deacons, especially to thy servants *N.,* our Metropolitan, and *N.,* our Bishop, that by their life and doctrine they may set forth thy true and living Word, and rightly and duly administer thy Holy Sacraments;

Hear us, we beseech thee.

That it may please thee to guide and prosper all those who are labouring for the spread of thy Gospel among the

167

nations, and to enlighten with thy Spirit all places of education and learning;

Hear us, we beseech thee.

That it may please thee that through thy heavenly benediction we may be saved from dearth and famine, and may with thankful hearts enjoy the fruits of the earth in their season;

Hear us, we beseech thee.

That it may please thee to give to all thy people thy heavenly grace; and specially to this congregation here present; that, with meek heart and due reverence, they may hear, and receive thy holy Word; truly serving thee in holiness and righteousness all the days of their life;

Hear us, we beseech thee.

That it may please thee of thy goodness, O Lord, to comfort and succour all them, who in this transitory life are in trouble, sorrow, need, sickness, or any other adversity;

Hear us, we beseech thee.

That it may please thee to grant to all thy servants departed this life in thy faith and fear, mercy, everlasting light, and peace;

Hear us, we beseech thee.

That it may please thee to give us grace that we may be partakers of thy heavenly kingdom with all thy Saints, holy Patriarchs, Prophets, Apostles, and Martyrs;

Hear us, we beseech thee.

The Litany ended, the Priest shall say:

Let us pray.

ALMIGHTY God, the fountain of all wisdom, who knowest our necessities before we ask, and our ignorance in asking; We beseech thee to have compassion upon our infirmities; and those things, which for our unworthiness we dare not, and for our blindness we cannot ask, vouchsafe to give us, for the worthiness of thy Son Jesus Christ our Lord. *Amen.*

THE CONSECRATION

Then the Priest, turning to the people, shall say:

The Lord be with you;
Answer. And with thy spirit.
Priest. Lift up your hearts;
Answer. We lift them up unto the Lord.
Priest. Let us give thanks unto our Lord God;
Answer. It is meet and right so to do.

And turning again to the Altar, the Priest shall proceed saying:

IT is very meet, right, and our bounden duty, that we should at all times, and in all places, give thanks unto thee, O Lord, Holy Father, Almighty, Everlasting God.

Here shall follow the Proper Preface, according to the time (see pp. 177–180), if there be any specially appointed; or else immediately shall follow:

THEREFORE with angels and archangels and with all the company of heaven, we laud and magnify thy glorious name; evermore praising thee, and saying,

Holy, holy, holy, Lord God of hosts, heaven and earth are full of thy glory. Glory be to thee, O Lord most High.

Then shall the Priest proceed saying:

HOLY in truth art thou, Father Almighty, Eternal King, and in thine every gift and work thou dost reveal thy holiness unto men. Holy is thine only-begotten Son, our Saviour Jesus Christ, through whom thou didst frame the worlds; and holy is thine ever-blessed Spirit, who searcheth out all things, yea, the deep things of thee, O God.

Even as thou thyself art holy, so also didst thou create man in thine own image that he might dwell in holiness before thee; and when he transgressed thy commandments, thou didst not abandon him, but didst chasten him as a merciful Father; thou spakest unto him through the law and by the prophets, and, when the fulness of time was come, thou spakest by thine only-begotten Son, whom thou didst send forth into the world to take our nature upon him, that he might renew thine image within us;

169

Who, suffering death upon the Cross for our redemption, made there (by his one oblation of himself once offered) a full, perfect, and sufficient sacrifice, oblation, and reconciliation, for the sins of the whole world; and did institute, and in his Holy Gospel command us to continue, a perpetual memorial of that his precious death until his coming again.

For, in the same night that he was betrayed, he *took Bread; and when he had given thanks to thee, O Father Almighty, he blessed it and *brake it, and gave it to his disciples, saying, Take, eat, *this is my Body which is given for you; Do this in remembrance of me.

a Here the Priest is to take the Bread into his hands:

b And here to break the Bread:

c And here to lay his hand upon all the Bread.

Likewise after supper he *took the Cup; and when he had given thanks to thee, he blessed it and gave it to them, saying, Drink ye all of this; for *this is my Blood of the New Covenant, which is shed for you and for many for the remission of sins; Do this, as oft as ye shall drink it, in remembrance of me.

d Here he is to take the Cup into his hand:

e And here to lay his hand upon every vessel in which there is any Wine to be consecrated.

Wherefore, O heavenly Father, we thy humble servants, having in remembrance the precious death and passion of thy dear Son, his mighty resurrection, his ascension into heaven, and his session in glory, and looking for his coming again; according to his holy institution, do celebrate, and set forth before thy Divine Majesty with these thy gifts, the memorial which he hath commanded us to make, rendering unto thee most hearty thanks for the innumerable benefits which he hath procured unto us.

And we beseech thee most merciful Father, to hear us, and to send thy Holy Spirit upon us and upon these thy gifts, that they, being blessed and hallowed by his life-giving power, may be unto us the Body and Blood of thy most dearly beloved Son, to the end that we, receiving the same, may be sanctified both in body and soul, and preserved unto life everlasting.

And we entirely desire thy fatherly goodness mercifully

to accept this our sacrifice of praise and thanksgiving; most humbly beseeching thee to grant, that by the merits and death of thy Son Jesus Christ, and through faith in his blood, we and all thy whole Church may obtain remission of our sins, and all other benefits of his passion.

And here we offer and present unto thee, O Lord, ourselves, our souls and bodies, to be a reasonable, holy, and living sacrifice unto thee: humbly beseeching thee, that all we, who are partakers of this Holy Communion, may be fulfilled with thy grace and heavenly benediction.

And although we be unworthy, through our manifold sins, to offer unto thee any sacrifice, yet we beseech thee to accept this our bounden duty and service; not weighing our merits, but pardoning our offences;

Through Jesus Christ our Lord, by whom, and with whom, in the unity of the Holy Ghost, all honour and glory be unto thee, O Father Almighty, world without end. *Amen.*

Let us pray.

As our Saviour Christ hath commanded and taught us, we are bold to say:

OUR Father, which art in heaven, Hallowed be thy name; Thy kingdom come; Thy will be done; In earth as it is in heaven. Give us this day our daily bread. And forgive us our trespasses, As we forgive them that trespass against us. And lead us not into temptation; But deliver us from evil: For thine is the kingdom, The power, and the glory, For ever and ever. Amen.

Then shall the Priest say:

The peace of the Lord be alway with you.
Answer. And with thy spirit.

Here the Priest and people shall say or sing:

HOSANNA in the highest. Blessed is he that cometh in the name of the Lord:
Hosanna in the highest.

Then shall silence be kept for a space.

THE COMMUNION

Then shall the Priest, kneeling down at the Lord's Table, say in the name of all them that shall receive the Holy Communion:

Let us pray.

WE do not presume to come to this thy Table, O merciful Lord, trusting in our own righteousness, but in thy manifold and great mercies. We are not worthy so much as to gather up the crumbs under thy Table. But thou art the same Lord, whose property is always to have mercy: Grant us therefore, gracious Lord, so to eat the Flesh of thy dear Son Jesus Christ, and to drink his Blood, that our sinful bodies may be made clean by his Body, and our souls washed through his most precious Blood, and that we may evermore dwell in him, and he in us. *Amen.*

Here shall follow this Anthem (which may be said or sung) the Priest standing; immediately after which or during which the Priest shall make his Communion.

O LAMB of God that takest away the sins of the world, Have mercy upon us (*or, at Requiems and funerals,* Grant them rest).

O Lamb of God that takest away the sins of the world, Have mercy upon us (*or, at Requiems and funerals,* Grant them rest).

O Lamb of God that takest away the sins of the world, Grant us thy peace (*or, at Requiems and funerals,* Grant them rest eternal).

The Priest shall receive the Communion in both kinds, saying when he partaketh of the consecrated Bread: THE BODY OF CHRIST, THE BREAD OF LIFE; *and, when he partaketh of the Cup:* THE BLOOD OF CHRIST, THE CHALICE OF LIFE; *and to whomsoever the Communion be administered, these same words shall be used therewith.*

The Priest, after he has himself received the Communion, turning to the people shall say to them that come to receive the Holy Communion:

DRAW near with faith, and take this Holy Sacrament to your comfort.

During Communion time Anthems and Hymns may be sung.

And when all have communicated, the Priest shall return to the Altar and shall reverently consume what remaineth of the consecrated Elements, and thereafter he shall cleanse the sacred vessels after the usual manner, and again cover them with a veil.

During this a Psalm or Hymn may be sung.

THE THANKSGIVING

Then shall the Priest say:

The Lord be with you.
Answer. And with thy spirit.

Then shall the Priest give thanks to God in the name of all them that have communicated, the Deacon first saying:

Let us give thanks unto God who hath refreshed us with food from his heavenly Table.

ALMIGHTY and everliving God, we most heartily thank thee, for that thou dost vouchsafe to feed us, who have duly received these holy mysteries, with the spiritual food of the most precious Body and Blood of thy Son our Saviour Jesus Christ; and dost assure us thereby of thy favour and goodness towards us; and that we are very members incorporate in the mystical body of thy Son, which is the blessed company of all faithful people; and are also heirs through hope of thy everlasting kingdom, by the merits of the most precious death and passion of thy dear Son. And we most humbly beseech thee, O heavenly Father, so to assist us with thy grace, that we may continue in that holy fellowship, and do all such good works as thou hast prepared for us to walk in; through Jesus Christ our Lord, to whom, with thee and the Holy Ghost, be all honour and glory, world without end. *Amen.*

Other prayers may be said here.

Here shall be said or sung the Gloria in Excelsis on Sundays (except in Advent, and on the Sundays from Septuagesima to Palm Sunday inclusive) and other Greater Feasts throughout the year, if it has not already been said or sung in the Introduction.

If the Gloria in Excelsis has already been said or sung, a Psalm or Hymn may be sung instead.

[*For the alternative see p.* 182.]

GLORY be to God on high, and in earth peace, good will towards men. We praise thee, we bless thee, we worship thee, we glorify thee, we give thanks to thee for thy great glory, O Lord God, heavenly King, God the Father Almighty.

O Lord, the only-begotten Son Jesu Christ; O Lord God, Lamb of God, Son of the Father, that takest away the sins of the world, have mercy upon us. Thou that takest away the sins of the world, have mercy upon us. Thou that takest away the sins of the world, receive our prayer. Thou that sittest at the right hand of God the Father, have mercy upon us.

For thou only art holy; thou only art the Lord; thou only, O Christ, with the Holy Ghost, art most high in the glory of God the Father. Amen.

Then the Priest (or the Bishop if he be present) shall let them depart with this Blessing.

THE peace of God, which passeth all understanding, keep your hearts and minds in the knowledge and love of God, and of his Son Jesus Christ our Lord: and the blessing of God Almighty, the Father, the Son, and the Holy Ghost, be amongst you and remain with you always. *Amen.*

And, the people being thus dismissed, the Priest and those with him in the sanctuary shall forthwith return to the sacristy.

THE ORDER FOR A SECOND CONSECRATION

If the consecrated Bread or Wine be all spent before all have communicated, the Priest shall consecrate more in both kinds, saying:

OUR Lord Jesus Christ, in the same night that he was betrayed, *a*took Bread; and when he had given thanks to thee, O Father Almighty, he blessed it and *b*brake it, and gave it to his disciples, saying, Take, eat, *c*this is my Body which is given for you; Do this in remembrance of me.

a Here the Priest is to take the Bread into his hands:

b And here to break the Bread:

c And here to lay his hand upon all the Bread.

Likewise after supper he ^dtook the Cup; and when he had given thanks to thee, he blessed it and gave it to them, saying, Drink ye all of this; for ^ethis is my Blood of the New Covenant, which is shed for you and for many for the remission of sins; Do this, as oft as ye shall drink it, in remembrance of me.

> ^d *Here he is to take the Cup into his hand:*
>
> ^e *And here to lay his hand upon every vessel in which there is any Wine to be consecrated.*

We beseech thee, therefore, most merciful Father, to hear us, and to send thy Holy Spirit upon us and upon these thy gifts, that they, being blessed and hallowed by his life-giving power, may be unto us the Body and Blood of thy most dearly beloved Son, to the end that we, receiving the same, may be sanctified both in body and soul, and preserved unto life everlasting. *Amen.*

SENTENCES FOR SPECIAL OCCASIONS

to be sung as Introits or said or sung at the Offertory.

ADVENT. Rejoice greatly, O daughter of Zion; shout, O daughter of Jerusalem: behold, thy King cometh unto thee.
Zechariah 9. 9.

CHRISTMAS. Unto us a child is born, unto us a son is given. *Isaiah* 9. 6.

EPIPHANY. All kings shall fall down before him: all nations shall do him service. *Psalm* 72. 11.

PRESENTATION. I will fill this house with glory, saith the Lord of hosts. *Haggai* 2. 7.

ANNUNCIATION. How beautiful upon the mountains are the feet of him that bringeth good tidings, that publisheth peace, that bringeth good tidings of good, that publisheth salvation; that saith unto Zion, Thy God reigneth! *Isaiah* 52. 7.

LENT. Rend your heart, and not your garments, and turn unto the Lord your God: for he is gracious and full of compassion. *Joel* 2. 13.

PASSIONTIDE. Thy rebuke hath broken my heart; I am full of heaviness: I looked for some to have pity on me, but there was no man, neither found I any to comfort me.
Psalm 69. 21.

MAUNDY THURSDAY. He shall feed me in a green pasture: and lead me forth beside the waters of comfort. *Psalm* 23. 2.

EASTER. Christ hath been raised from the dead, the first-fruits of them that are asleep. Alleluia. 1 *Corinthians* 15. 20.

ROGATION DAYS. Verily, verily, I say unto you, if ye shall ask anything of the Father, he will give it you in my name. *St. John* 16. 23.

ASCENSION. Lift up your heads, O ye gates, and be ye lift up, ye everlasting doors: and the King of glory shall come in. Alleluia. *Psalm* 24. 9.

WHITSUNDAY. I will pour out my spirit upon all flesh. Alleluia. *Joel* 2. 28.

TRINITY. Who shall not fear, O Lord, and glorify thy name? for thou only art holy. *Revelation* 15. 4.

EMBER DAYS. The harvest is plenteous, but the labourers are few: pray ye therefore the Lord of the harvest, that he send forth labourers into his harvest. *St. Luke* 10. 2.

TRANSFIGURATION. We all, with unveiled face reflecting as a mirror the glory of the Lord, are transformed into the same image from glory to glory, even as from the Lord the Spirit. 2 *Corinthians* 3. 18.

SAINTS' DAYS. All thy works praise thee, O Lord: and thy saints give thanks unto thee. *Psalm* 145. 10.

AT INTERCESSIONS FOR MISSIONS. Go ye and make disciples of all the nations, baptizing them into the name of the Father and of the Son and of the Holy Ghost: teaching them to observe all things whatsoever I commanded you: and lo, I am with you alway, even unto the end of the world. *St. Matthew* 28. 19,20.

At Memorials of the Departed. None of us liveth to himself, and none dieth to himself. For whether we live, we live unto the Lord; or whether we die, we die unto the Lord: whether we live therefore, or die, we are the Lord's.

Romans 14. 7,8.

Dedication Festival. The glory of this latter house shall be greater than of the former, saith the Lord of hosts: and in this place will I give peace, saith the Lord of hosts.

Haggai 2. 9.

PROPER PREFACES

During Advent.

BECAUSE thou hast given salvation unto mankind through the coming of thy well-beloved Son in great humility, and by him wilt make all things new when he shall come again in his glorious Majesty to judge the world in righteousness.

Upon Christmas Day *and until the* Epiphany *and upon the Feast of the* Annunciation.

BECAUSE thou didst give Jesus Christ thine only Son to be born for our salvation: Who, by the operation of the Holy Ghost, was made very man of the substance of the Virgin Mary his mother: And that without spot of sin, to make us clean from all sin.

Upon the Epiphany *and seven days after.*

THROUGH Jesus Christ our Lord: Who in substance of our mortal flesh, manifested forth his glory: That he might bring all men out of darkness into his own marvellous light.

Upon the Feast of the Presentation.

BECAUSE thy blessed Son Jesus Christ our Lord, born of a woman, born under the Law, was presented in the Temple, and revealed to thy servants as a light to lighten the Gentiles and the glory of thy people Israel.

Upon Ash Wednesday *and until* Passion Sunday.

BECAUSE thou hast given us the spirit of discipline, that we may triumph over the flesh, and live no longer unto ourselves but unto him who died for us and rose again.

Upon Passion Sunday *and until the* Thursday before Easter.

THROUGH Jesus Christ our Lord: Who, being found in fashion as a man, humbled himself and became obedient unto death, even the death of the Cross, that, being lifted up from the earth, he might draw all men unto him.

Upon the Thursday before Easter *and upon a* Thanksgiving for the Institution of Holy Communion.

THROUGH Jesus Christ our Lord: Who having loved his own that were in the world loved them unto the end: And on the night before he suffered, sitting at meat with his disciples, did institute these holy mysteries: That we, redeemed by his death and quickened by his resurrection, might be partakers of his divine nature.

Upon Easter Day *and until* Ascension Day.

BUT chiefly are we bound to praise thee for the glorious resurrection of thy Son Jesus Christ our Lord: For he is the very Paschal Lamb, which was offered for us, and hath taken away the sin of the world; Who by his death hath destroyed death, and by his rising to life again hath restored to us everlasting life.

Upon Ascension Day *and until* Whitsunday.

THROUGH thy most dearly beloved Son Jesus Christ our Lord: Who after his most glorious resurrection manifestly appeared to all his Apostles: And in their sight ascended up into heaven to prepare a place for us; That where he is, thither we might also ascend, and reign with him in glory.

Upon Whitsunday *and six days after.*

THROUGH Jesus Christ our Lord: Who after that he had ascended up far above all the heavens, and was set down at the right hand of thy Majesty: Did pour forth upon the Church thy Holy and Life-giving Spirit: That through his power the everlasting gospel might go forth into all the world: Whereby we have been brought out of darkness and error into the clear light and true knowledge of thee, and of thy Son our Saviour Jesus Christ.

Upon the Feast of Trinity *only.*

WHO with thine only-begotten Son and the Holy Ghost art one God, one Lord, in Trinity of Persons and in Unity of Substance: For that which we believe of thy glory, the same we believe of thy Son and of the Holy Ghost, without any difference or inequality.

Upon the Feast of the Transfiguration.

BECAUSE the divine glory of the Incarnate Word shone forth upon the Holy Mount before the witnesses of his majesty: And thine own voice from heaven proclaimed thy beloved Son.

Upon All Saints' Day *and the Feasts of* Apostles, Evangelists, *and* St. John Baptist's Nativity, *except when the Proper Preface of any Principal Feast is appointed.*

WHO in the righteousness of thy Saints hast given us an ensample of godly living, and in their blessedness a glorious pledge of the hope of our calling: That, being compassed about with so great a cloud of witnesses, we may run with patience the race that is set before us: And with them receive the crown of glory that fadeth not away.

Upon the Consecration of Bishops, *and the* Ordination of Priests *and* Deacons *and upon* Ember Days.

THROUGH Jesus Christ our Lord, the great Shepherd of the sheep: who, for the feeding and guidance of his flock, did appoint divers Orders of Ministers in his Church.

At Memorials of the Departed.

THROUGH Jesus Christ our Lord: Who hath brought life and immortality to light, that we, who are burdened by the weight of sin and death, might not sorrow as those who have no hope: Because we know that when our earthly tabernacle is dissolved we have a better habitation.

Upon the Consecration of a Church, *or upon the*
Feast of its Dedication.

WHO, though the heaven of heavens cannot contain thee and thy glory is in all the world: Dost deign to hallow places for thy worship, and in them dost pour forth gifts of grace upon thy faithful people.

Upon any Sunday in the year for which no other
Proper Preface is appointed.

THROUGH Jesus Christ our Lord: Who on the first day of the week did rise from the dead, that we might live in him by the power of the Holy Ghost.

In place of the Prayer and the Litany on page 167, *the following Offertory Prayer*
may be used, the Priest first saying:

Let us pray.

ALMIGHTY and everliving God, who by thy holy Apostle has taught us to make prayers, and supplications, and to give thanks, for all men: We humbly beseech thee most mercifully to accept our (alms and) oblations, and to receive these our prayers, which we offer unto thy Divine Majesty; beseeching thee to inspire continually the universal Church with the spirit of truth, unity, and concord. And grant, that all they that do confess thy holy name may agree in the truth of thy holy Word, and live in unity, and godly love.

We beseech thee also to lead all nations in the paths of righteousness and peace; and so to direct all kings and rulers, especially thy servant *George*, our king, that under them the world may be godly and quietly governed.

Give grace, O heavenly Father, to all Bishops, Priests, and Deacons, especially to thy servants *N*, our Metropolitan, and *N*, our Bishop, that by their life and doctrine they may set forth thy true and living Word, and rightly and duly administer thy holy Sacraments.

Guide and prosper, we pray thee, all those who are labouring for the spread of thy Gospel among the nations, and enlighten with thy Spirit all places of education and learning; that the whole world may be filled with the knowledge of thy truth.

We entreat thee also, O Lord, that through thy heavenly benediction we may be saved from dearth and famine, and may with thankful hearts enjoy the fruits of the earth in their season.

And to all thy people give thy heavenly grace; and specially to this congregation here present; that, with meek heart and due reverence, they may hear, and receive thy holy Word; truly serving thee in holiness and righteousness all the days of their life.

And we most humbly beseech thee of thy goodness, O Lord, to comfort and succour all them, who in this transitory life are in trouble, sorrow, need, sickness, or any other adversity.

We commend to thy fatherly goodness, O Lord, all thy servants departed this life in thy faith and fear, beseeching thee to grant them mercy, everlasting light, and peace.

And here we give thee most high praise and hearty thanks for all thy Saints, who have been the chosen vessels of thy grace, and lights of the world in their several generations; and we pray, that rejoicing in their fellowship, and following their good examples, we may be partakers with them of thy heavenly kingdom.

Grant this, O Father, for Jesus Christ's sake, our Advocate and only Mediator; who liveth and reigneth with thee in the unity of the Holy Ghost, ever one God, world without end. *Amen.*

Then shall the Priest proceed with the Consecration as on page 169.

The Gloria in Excelsis may be said or sung in the following form:

GLORY be to God on high, and in earth peace, good will towards men. We praise thee, we bless thee, we worship thee, we glorify thee; We give thanks to thee for thy great glory, O Lord God, heavenly King, God the Father Almighty, and to thee, O God, the only-begotten Son Jesu Christ, and to thee, O God, the Holy Ghost.

O Lord, the only-begotten Son Jesu Christ; O Lord God, Lamb of God, Son of the Father, that takest away the sins of the world, have mercy upon us. Thou that takest away the sins of the world, receive our prayer. Thou that sittest at the right hand of God the Father, have mercy upon us.

For thou only art holy, thou only art the Lord; thou only, O Christ, art most high in the glory of God the Father. Amen.

APPENDIX I

Deviations of the IRISH rite from the English 1662

THIS order (1926) corresponds closely with the English Rite of 1662, but with the following main variations:

The disciplinary rubrics before the opening of the service are reduced to a single rubric of greatly diminished size and scope, thus:

If the Minister shall have knowledge or reasonable ground to believe that any person who is living in open and notorious sin intends to come to the Holy Communion, so that scandal would thereby arise, he shall privately admonish him not to presume to come to the Lord's Table till the cause of offence shall have been removed; and in every such case the Minister shall have regard to the Canons relating thereto.

and an initial direction is given that '*The Minister shall say the Service following in a distinct and audible voice*'.

Permission is given to substitute for the Ten Commandments (which, however, shall be said at least once on the Lord's Day, and on the great festivals, when there is a celebration of Holy Communion) the Summary of the Law, of which the text agrees with the Canadian form.

No Collect for the King is to be said '*when the King has been prayed for in any Service used along with this Office, or when the Prayer* For the whole state of Christ's Church *is said*'.

The rubric preceding the Epistle and Gospel provides for the reading of each of these lessons by 'one of the Ministers'. After the announcement of the Gospel '*may be said or sung*, Glory be to thee, O Lord. *And after the Gospel ended*, Thanks be to thee, O Lord, *or* Hallelujah'.

After the Offertory Sentences (which show considerable correspondence with those of the English use of 1928, with the addition of Deut. 16. 16,17 and Prov. 19. 17) there is added

After which may be said one of these following:

(*For* CHRISTMAS)

Ye know the grace of our Lord Jesus Christ, that, though he was rich, yet for your sakes he became poor, that ye through his poverty might be rich.   *2 Cor.* 8. 9.

(*For* EASTER)

Christ our passover is sacrificed for us: therefore let us keep the east.   1 *Cor.* 5. 7,8.

(*For* ASCENSION)

When he ascended up on high, he led captivity captive, and gave gifts unto men.   *Eph.* 4. 8.

(*For* WHITSUNTIDE)

God hath sealed us, and given the earnest of the Spirit in our hearts.   2 *Cor.* 1. 22.

(*Upon* TRINITY SUNDAY)

Now unto the King eternal, immortal, invisible, the only wise God, be honour and glory for ever and ever. Amen.   1 *Tim.* 1. 17.

Thine, O Lord, is the greatness, and the power, and the glory, and the victory, and the majesty; for all that is in the heaven and in the earth is thine; thine is the kingdom, O Lord, and thou art exalted as head above all. Now therefore, our God, we thank thee, and praise thy glorious Name; for all things come of thee, and of thine own have we given thee.   1 *Chron.* 29. 11,13,14.

The rubric before the first Long Exhortation appears thus:

When the Minister giveth warning for the celebration of the Holy Communion, he may read this Exhortation following, or such part of it as he thinketh most convenient.

And before the third Long Exhortation:

At the time of the celebration of the Communion (those who do not intend to communicate having had opportunity to withdraw) the Communicants being conveniently placed for the receiving of the holy Sacrament, the Priest shall say this Exhortation.

Note, that if this Exhortation be not read at the time of the celebration of the Communion, it shall, nevertheless, be read to the people by the Curate at such times as he shall think fit, and at least three times in the year.

In the Exhortations one or two archaic words are changed (such as 'ghostly' to 'spiritual') and, as in the Canadian rite, from the third Exhortation is omitted the sentence 'we kindle God's wrath against us . . . sundry kinds of death'.

At the Preface, no rubric requires the omission of the words 'Holy Father' on Trinity Sunday. The Proper Preface for Whitsuntide is in line with the English 1928 and South African forms thus:

THROUGH Jesus Christ our Lord; who, after that he had ascended up far above all the heavens, and was set down at thy right hand, did as at this time pour forth upon the children of adoption thy holy and life-giving Spirit; that through his glorious power the joy of the everlasting Gospel might come abroad into all the world; whereby we have been brought out of darkness and error into the clear light and true knowledge of thee, and of thy Son Jesus Christ.

That for Trinity Sunday agrees with the Scottish, American, and South African uses.

The rubric before the Prayer of Consecration defines the position of the Priest as '*standing at the north side of The Table*', and the prayer itself is articulated into three paragraphs thus 'Almighty God . . .', 'Hear us . . .', 'Who in the same night . . .'.

Permission is given to say either or both the Prayer of Oblation and the Prayer of Thanksgiving, and these are followed by the rubric '*Then, all standing up, shall be said or sung Gloria in excelsis, as followeth:*'.

'*Collects which may be said after the Collect of the Day, or before the Blessing, at the discretion of the Minister*' include, in addition to those at the end of the English 1662 rite, a generalized version of the penultimate prayer at the Burial of the Dead, 'Most merciful Father . . .' from the Ordering of Priests, the Prayer for Missions 'O God who hast made of one blood . . .', and the two Embertide Prayers, the whole section concluding thus:

A Prayer which may be used after the collection, when there is no Communion.

ALMIGHTY God, we humbly beseech thee to accept the offerings which we have presented unto thee, and mercifully to receive our supplications and prayers; and grant, that those things, which we have faithfully asked according to thy will, may effectually be obtained, to the relief of our necessity, and to the setting forth of thy glory; through Jesus Christ our Lord. *Amen.*

¶ *Upon Sundays and Holy-days (if there be no Communion) all shall be said as appointed up to the Prayer* [For the whole state of Christ's Church militant here in earth]; *which Prayer may in such case be said, or omitted, at the discretion of the Minister; and then shall follow one or more of the Collects; concluding with the Blessing.*

¶ *And there shall be no celebration of the Lord's Supper, except there be three (or two at the least) of the people to communicate with the Priest.*

¶ *And in Cathedral and Collegiate Churches, and Colleges, where there are many Priests and Deacons, they shall all receive the Communion with the Priest every Sunday at the least, except they have a reasonable cause to the contrary.*

¶ *On occasions sanctioned by the Ordinary, this Office may begin with the Collect, Epistle, and Gospel.*

¶ *And to take away all occasion of dissension, and superstition, which any person hath or might have concerning the Bread and Wine, the Bread shall be such as is usual to be eaten; but the best and purest Wheat Bread that conveniently may be gotten.*

¶ *And if any remain of the Bread and Wine which was consecrated, it shall not be carried out of the Church, but the Priest and such other of the Communicants as he shall then call unto him, shall, immediately after the Blessing, reverently eat and drink the same.*

¶ *All Ministers shall exhort their people to communicate frequently. And every Parishioner shall from time to time be exhorted to contribute regularly of his substance to the maintenance of the worship of God, according as God shall prosper him.*

¶ *And when, by reason of numbers, it is inconvenient to address to each Communicant, separately, the words appointed to be said on delivering the Bread and the Cup, the words may, with the consent of the Ordinary, be said once to as many as shall together kneel for receiving the Communion at the holy Table: provided that the words shall be said separately to any Communicant so desiring it.*

¶ *After the Divine Service ended, the money given at the Offertory shall be disposed of to such pious and charitable uses as the Minister and Church-wardens shall think fit. Wherein if they disagree, it shall be disposed of as the Ordinary shall appoint.*

and the Black Rubric.

APPENDIX II

Deviations of the CANADIAN rite from the English 1662

THIS order (1921) corresponds closely with the English Rite of 1662 with the following exceptions. (One or two archaisms of language are adjusted such as 'living' for 'lively', and 'impartially' for 'indifferently'.)

Permission is given to substitute for the Ten Commandments the Summary of the Law thus:

¶ *Or, he may rehearse instead of the Ten Commandments (which however shall be said at least once on Sunday, and on the great Festivals, when there is a Celebration of the holy Communion, and that always at the chief Service of the day), our Blessed Lord's summary of the Law as followeth.*

Hear what our Lord Jesus Christ saith.

THOU shalt love the Lord thy God with all thy heart, and with all thy soul, and with all thy mind. This is the first and great commandment. And the second is like unto it; Thou shalt love thy neighbour as thyself. On these two commandments hang all the Law and the Prophets.

People. Lord, have mercy upon us, and write both these thy laws in our hearts, we beseech thee.

After directions for announcing the Gospel there follows this rubric:

¶ *Here shall be sung or said,*
Glory be to thee, O Lord.

And, the Gospel ended, the people shall in like manner sing or say,
Thanks be to thee, O Lord.

¶ *Then shall be sung or said this Creed following, the people still standing as before.*

Three Offertory Sentences are added from 1 Chron. 29. 14, Exod. 35. 21, and Acts 20. 35.

The first Long Exhortation is introduced thus:

When the Minister giveth warning for the Celebration of the holy Communion, (which he shall always do upon the Sunday, or some Holy-day, immediately preceding,) after the Sermon or Homily ended, or else after the Nicene Creed, he may read this Exhortation following, or the first paragraph thereof, at his discretion; provided always, that he read the whole Exhortation upon some Sunday before Christmas Day, Easter Day, and Whitsunday, the people all standing.

and from its text is omitted the warning 'lest, after the taking of that holy Sacrament, the devil . . . destruction both of body and soul'. The third Long Exhortation is made optional, and from it is omitted the sentence 'we kindle God's wrath against us . . . sundry kinds of death'.

A Proper Preface is appointed for the Epiphany and seven days after (the text as in the Scottish Liturgy), and the Whitsuntide Proper Preface refers to 'the gift of tongues'.

At the discretion of the Minister both the Prayer of Oblation and the Prayer of Thanksgiving may be used.

The minimum number to communicate with the Priest is reduced to three (or two at least); and provision is made that every parishioner shall contribute regularly of his substance to the maintenance of the worship of God, according as God shall prosper him.

APPENDIX III

An Essay in Liturgical Construction

The observations printed below were drawn from the late Bishop Walter Howard Frere in 1918 in relation to the South African revision of the Eucharistic Office. They are confined to the Anaphora and open with a discussion of the verbal adjustment by which Sanctus should (to use his own language) be 'bonded in' to the Eucharistic Prayer, particularly the words by which a logical link should be forged between the end of Sanctus and the resumption of the Preamble.

IN the other Latin liturgies the link normally appeared in the form 'Vere sanctus', or more fully 'Vere sanctus et vere benedictus'. In the bulk of Gallican 'Post-Sanctus' prayers it is our Lord who is spoken of as 'Vere sanctus' and in the third person, since of course the prayer is addressed to the Father. This no doubt is the natural use of the quotation. It must be regarded as a momentary turning aside to give a spontaneous expression of homage to our Lord. If the precedent of the majority of the 'Post-Sanctus' prayers is followed, the return to addressing the Father will be made by some such phrase as this: 'Vere sanctus vere benedictus Dominus noster J. C. Filius tuus qui (*or* quem)', etc. But there is a good number of cases in which the words 'Vere sanctus', and even 'Vere benedictus' are used of the Father and to the Father, and among them are some of the most important, e.g. at Easter in the Mozarabic Rite (*Liber Mozarabicus Sacramentorum*, Ferotin, 626)

> 'Vere sanctus et benedictus es, Deus Pater omnipotens, qui Dominum nostrum J. C. Filium tuum in assumptione humanitatis mortem fecisti subire, ut', etc.

Again in the *Missae Quotidianae* (which often represent the earlier and more normal forms) we find:

> 'Vere sanctus et vere benedictus in excelsis, omnipotens tu Deus Pater, cujus munere cunctis hominibus imaginis tuae dignitas conceditur in natura', etc.

Or again in the Advent mass of the *Missale Gallicanum* (Neale and Forbes, *Gallican Liturgies*, 157):

> 'Vere sanctus, vere benedictus, Domine Deus Pater omnipotens,

189

salus credentium, et omnium Redemptor in Christo. Per quem te deprecamur et quaesumus: ut hanc oblationem', etc.

This form of link therefore seems the more desirable one. The proposed form [of the South African Church[1]] links on the Consecration Prayer to the mistranslation of the Hosanna which ought to go. This link is a firmer and sounder one, for it connects with the *Sanctus* and *Benedictus* and pulls all together. Some such form as this seems therefore advisable:

'Holy in truth art thou, and blessed in truth, O Almighty God our heavenly Father, for that thou of thy tender mercy', &c.

which it will be observed agrees closely with the Easter prayer cited above.

The offering of the gifts is one of the undisplaced features of the Roman Canon; and if the model of that prayer is used for the 'remembrance' it may well be carried on to this clause also.

'Offerimus praeclarae majestati tuae de tuis donis ac datis hostiam puram, hostiam sanctam, hostiam immaculatam, panem sanctum vitae aeternae et calicem salutis perpetuae.'

This procedure is also common in the non-Roman Latin liturgies, e.g. in the *Missale Gothicum* (N. and F. 148):

'Memores gloriosissimi Domini passionis, et ab inferis resurrectionis, offerimus tibi, Domine, hanc immaculatam hostiam, rationalem hostiam, incruentam hostiam, hunc panem sanctum et calicem salutarem.'

Or this in the Mozarabic rite (*L.M.S.* 1288):

'Commemorantes ergo Redemptoris nostri praecepta, simulque passionem et in coelum ascensionem, offerimus tibi, Deus Pater omnipotens, haec dona et munera, et fidelium tuorum sacrificia illibata.'

Considering that this section leads on to the Invocation, it is desirable to approach that part of the prayer, round which dogmatic difficulties cluster, by a type of phrase which is common to both Roman and Gallican rites. The following is therefore suggested:

'Wherefore, O Lord, . . . and glory, we do offer unto thy divine majesty these sacred gifts and creatures of thine own, this holy bread of eternal life and this cup of everlasting salvation.'

[1] *Proposed Form of the South African Liturgy*, 1918.

The form which the mention of the Holy Spirit should take is to be called in some sense an 'Invocation', but the intervention of the Holy Spirit, where it is expressly mentioned has been described in a great variety of ways. Any restoration of this feature should follow one or other of the many shapes that this section has taken in Western Latin liturgy rather than be modelled on Eastern precedents.

(a) A direct invocation addressed to the Holy Spirit is rare, and these precedents should not be followed.

(b) Usually the appeal is made to the Father to bless what is being offered by the outpouring of the Holy Spirit (N. and F. 4, 8, 15):

> 'uti hoc sacrificium tua benedictione benedicas, et Sancti Spiritus tui rore perfundas.'

(c) Sometimes the prayer is that the Holy Spirit may descend (ib. 59, 153, 157):

> 'Descendat, Domine, in his sacrificiis tuae benedictionis coeternus et cooperator Paraclitus Spiritus.
>
> 'Descendat, precamur, omnipotens Deus, super haec, quae tibi offerimus, Verbum tuum sanctum, descendat inestimabilis gloriae tuae Spiritus.'

(d) Or more generally that the *divine power* may descend and consecrate (ib. 11):

> 'Descendat, Domine, plenitudo majestatis, divinitatis, pietatis, virtutis, benedictionis et gloriae tuae super hunc panem et super hunc calicem.'

(e) Or a combination of the two (ib. 135):

> 'ut descendat hic benedictio tua super hunc panem et calicem, in transformatione Spiritus tui Sancti.'

(f) Another type speaks of the *sending* of the Holy Spirit (ib. 74):

> 'ut immittere digneris Spiritum tuum Sanctum super haec sollemnia.'

(g) Sometimes a mention of all of the persons of the Holy Trinity is made (ib. 146):

> 'Per quem te, Pater omnipotens, deprecamur, ut suprapositaltario tuo munera laetus aspicias, atque haec omnia obumbres Sancti Filii tui Spiritus.'

It is hardly possible to decide which should be the type of invocation to be adopted, without first considering also the ensuing clause, descriptive of the effect of the coming of the Holy Spirit. In some instances the description is brief and general; in others it is more detailed, and exposes more explicitly the 'change' involved in Consecration, usually by some such word as *transfusio* or *transformatio*. The latter type is less likely to be thought suitable now, in view of the controversies which have arisen since these various formulas were penned; to restore such terms would only reopen controversy. The following examples of the former type may therefore serve better as guides. The simplest form, and a common one is this (ib. 4, 15, 99):

'ut [sacrificium] accipientibus universis legitima sit eucharistia (*or* eucharistia pura vera legitima) per Jesum', etc.

Another follows the phrase (ib. 11, 47, 74):

'ut fiat nobis legitima eucharistia',

but this is often followed by a description of the 'transformation'. Moreover, 'fiat nobis' anticipates the effect *on the Communicant*, a point which is provided for in our prayer at a later stage; and formulas which speak at this point of the effect on the communicant are not therefore the best for us to follow.

Another type speaks of the effect of the Holy Spirit's work in terms of sanctification. For example (*L.M.S.* 360, 627):

'Emitte Spiritum tuum de sanctis caelis tuis, quo sanctificetur oblata, suscipiantur vota, expientur delicta.'

Or

'Deferatur in ista sollemnia Spiritus tuus Sanctus, qui tam adstantis quam offerentis populi et oblata pariter et vota sanctificet.'

Again, there are other general descriptions of the Eucharistic significance of the Holy Spirit's work, which clash neither with the Eastern nor with the Western theories of consecration (*L.M.S.* 70, 617, 1191):

'Fac quaesumus hoc tui Corporis Sanguinisque mysterium, Spiritus tui rore sanctificatum, ad nostrarum remedium sumere animarum.'

Or,

'Ut hic tibi panis cum hoc calice oblatus in filii tui Corpus et Sanguinem te benedicente ditescat: ac, largo oris tui perfusus Spiritu, indulgentiam nobis omnium peccatorum largiatur et gratiam.'

Or,

> 'Sic hoc sacrificium respicere et sanctificare digneris, quod est verum Corpus et Sanguis D. N. J. C.'

What is required at this critical point is something which fulfils two conditions, (*a*) that it should be explicit as to the reality of the Consecration, and should therefore contrast the 'bread' and 'wine' with the consecrated Body and Blood; and (*b*) that it should do so in a way which avoids the controversy between East and West as to the moment, or operative words, of the Consecration. To follow Greek terms is therefore inadvisable. It is very doubtful whether these terms are early, for the 'primitive' character of the living Greek liturgies has been greatly overstated. While in general form they are perhaps more primitive than the Latin rites, they have undergone much more modification in detail during the early medieval period. And how far they are from the early form of the Invocation will be seen by comparing the third-century formula in the Hyppolytean Church Order.

Such passages as those cited seem to provide us with terms sufficiently definite, and also sufficiently indefinite; their adoption would point to some such formula as this:

> 'Entreating thee to send from high heaven thy Holy Spirit to sanctify our offerings, and to hallow these our vows, that by the dew of his grace this mystery of the Body and Blood of thy Son may be available for the healing of our souls.'

or this:

> 'May thy Holy Spirit descend upon these offerings, and hallow this oblation of the Body and Blood of thy Son Jesus Christ our Lord.'

Then the prayer would be continued:

> 'Thus we entirely desire thy fatherly goodness,' &c.

and the words 'that thy Holy Spirit may be poured upon us' would be omitted [from the '*Proposed Form*'].

The Lord's Prayer needs some special eucharistic ending. If the familiar doxology is *removed* from it in all other places where the prayer occurs, it might serve *here* in that capacity. But there is better precedent for a fresh piece of prayer linked on to the end of the Lord's Prayer, introduced by a repetition of the word 'Libera'. The briefest type is exhibited thus in one of the *Missae Dominicales* (N. and F. 144). 'Libera nos a malo omnipotens Deus, et custodi in bono, qui vivis,' etc., and some such incorporating prayer seems all the more necessary if, as now, the Lord's Prayer is sung by the congregation, and not, as once was the case, by the celebrant alone, the people replying 'Sed libera nos a malo'.

The suggestion has been made that the Prayer of Humble Access should be made a *Libera* prayer thus:

> 'Deliver us from all evil, and preserve us in all good, for we do not presume', &c.

There seems to be much to be said for this, for the words are familiar and suitable to the place, and would come much better here than in their present position. But a brief one has many points in its favour. There are plenty of precedents, and the Gallican formulas are very similar to the Roman. This also raises the question of the position to be occupied by the preparatory prayers for communicants. Granted that the set are kept together, or at least that the prayer of Humble Access is no longer intruded in the Canon, (1) Should the preparation be made before the Anaphora, or after? (2) Should the celebrant make his preparation with the communicants, or make a separate preparation before beginning the service?

These questions are open ones. I would only record a preference for the preparation being made jointly by celebrant and communicants, and being made before the Anaphora. The group of Exhortation, Confession, Absolution, and Comfortable Words and Prayer of Humble Access is too long to intercalate between the Consecration and Communion [as in South African *'Proposed Form'*]. If such prayers are to be interpolated in that place, they must be much briefer. As it is they place the celebrant in an undesirable position, having to go through so much movement and turning with the Holy Sacrament lying on the altar.

[W. H. F.]

The text resulting from the foregoing study would read thus:

HOLY in truth art thou, and blessed in truth, O Almighty God our heavenly Father, for that thou of thy tender mercy didst give thine only Son Jesus Christ to take our nature upon him, and to suffer death upon the cross for our redemption, who . . .[1] [words of Institution].

Wherefore, O Lord and heavenly Father, we thy humble servants, having in remembrance his blessed passion and precious death, his mighty resurrection and glorious ascension, do render unto thee most hearty thanks for the innumerable benefits procured unto us by the same; and, looking for his coming again with power and great glory, we do offer unto thy divine majesty these sacred gifts and creatures of thine own, this holy Bread of eternal life, and this Cup of everlasting salvation, entreating thee to send from high heaven thy Holy Spirit to sanctify our offerings, and to hallow these our vows; that by the dew of his grace this mystery of the Body and Blood of thy Son may be available for the healing of our souls.

Thus we entirely desire thy fatherly goodness . . .

Lord's Prayer.

Deliver us from all evil, O Almighty God, and keep us in all good, who livest and reignest . . .

[1] In the proposals which gave rise to these notes, the 1552 prayer 'Hear us . . . may be partakers of his most blessed Body and Blood' (referred to by Dr. Frere in *The Anaphora* as 'the intruded clause') was present, and remains a distinctive feature of the South African rite (Ed.).

195

PRINTED IN
GREAT BRITAIN
AT THE
UNIVERSITY PRESS
OXFORD
BY
JOHN JOHNSON
PRINTER
TO THE
UNIVERSITY